Learn How to Draw
Using Charcoal for Beginners

Mark Anthony Lingat
And
John Davidson

Learn to Draw
Book Series

Mendon Cottage Books
JD- Biz Publishing

Learn How to Draw Books for the Absolute Beginner

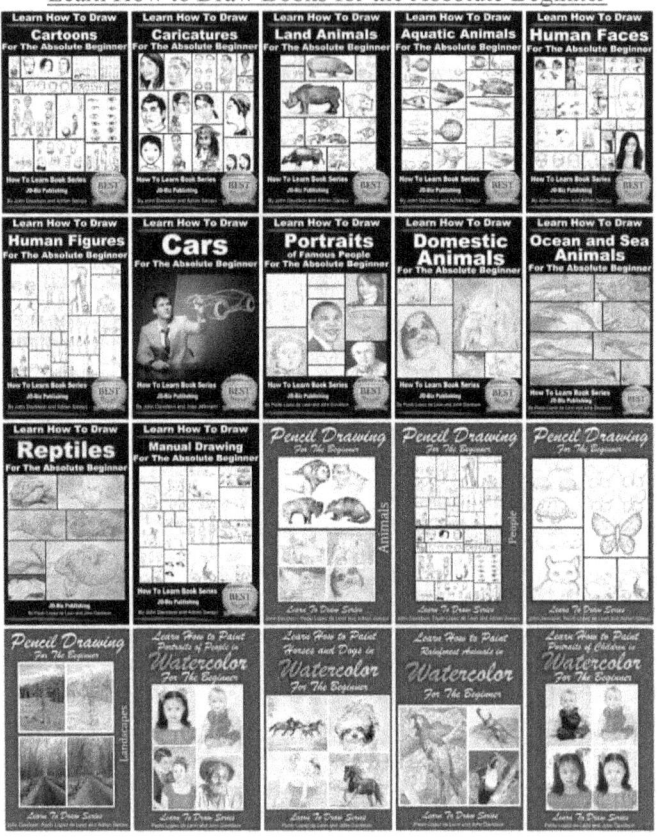

TABLE OF CONTENTS

Introduction 4
Materials: 5
Working Area 11
Do's and Don'ts.. 11
Still Life 12
Values of Shade.. 13
Drawing Light and Shadows.. 14
Exercise 1: Sphere 15
Still Life of a Sphere 22
Exercise 2: Metal Pot... 23
The Metal Pot... 29
Exercise 3: Fruits 31
Fruits.. 37
Drawing from Photographs 38
Tips to remember: 43
Author Bio.. 44
Publisher.. 47
Bonus Book.. 48
Learn How to Draw Portraits of 48
African Animals in Charcoal... 48
For the Beginner 48
Materials.. 52
Shaving the Charcoal 60
Rendering Using Charcoal... 61
Application 66
Drawing an Outline 66
Grid System... 66
Tracing Table or Light Table / Flexi-glass with Bendable Lamp.............. 67
Tips to Remember 67
Exercises 69
Zebra.. 69
Giraffe.. 76
Elephant.. 84
Baby Chimp 91
Lion 103
Author Bio.. 111

Introduction

When it comes to black and white drawing, no other medium is as rich and satisfying as charcoal. The velvety darks and the ability to create loose, gestural marks are what make charcoal so unique. This e-book "Learn How To Draw Using Charcoal For Beginners" will help you on how to start your enthusiasm in art. It seems that charcoal is one of the medium that it is hard to use, but this e-book makes it easier especially to those who are beginners. Even if you are not good enough in drawing I hope this will help you on how to draw in a basic principle. It doesn't matter what age are you, what matters most is you have desire to draw.

New artists are often encouraged to begin drawing with charcoal as soon as start life drawing. This is because charcoal is ideal for making a variety of different lines very quickly. You can smudge charcoal with your fingers or some paper to shade it, remove small sections quickly for highlights, or use an edge to create a hard line. Because new artists often have to practice drawing the same lines over and over again, using a versatile tool like charcoal allows the artist to produce a variety of effects to get the desired style quickly and without needing to take the time to select and reselect materials. Just follow the simple step-by-step instructions on how to draw and render using charcoal. I hope this will help you to improve and to develop your skills and talent in drawing. It also contains what materials you have to use and techniques in preparation so that it is easy for you to start. My advice is just practice more, research with the art you love and lastly, have fun and enjoy it!

Materials:

HB Pencils or Mechanical Pencils

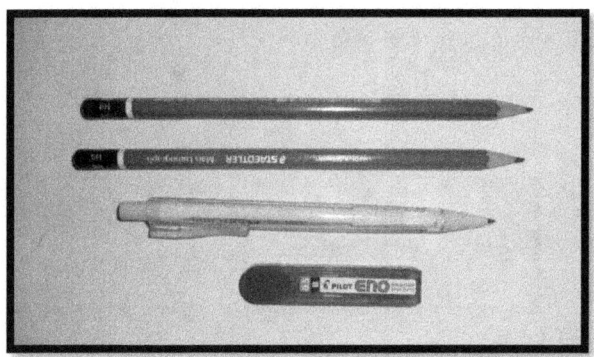

A pencil is a writing implement or art medium usually constructed of a narrow, solid pigment core inside a protective casing which prevents the core from being broken or leaving marks on the user's hand during use.
It is used when you are sketching or drawing your model to be rendered.
HB pencil is advisable for sketching because it has a soft lead that is easy to draw with paper. A mechanical pencil is also advisable because you don't need to sharpen the tip, but instead you have to change only the lead.

Charcoal Pencil

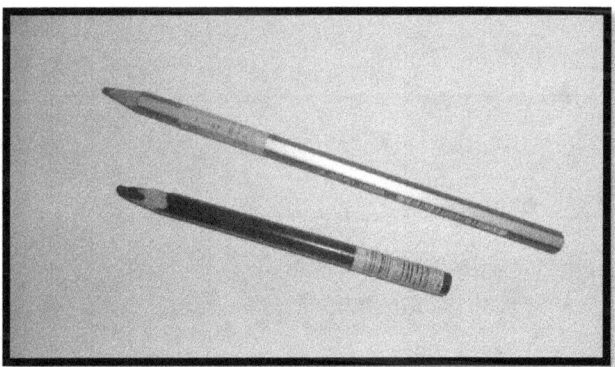

A strip or cylinder of artist's charcoal often in a slender wooden casing.

Charcoal Bars

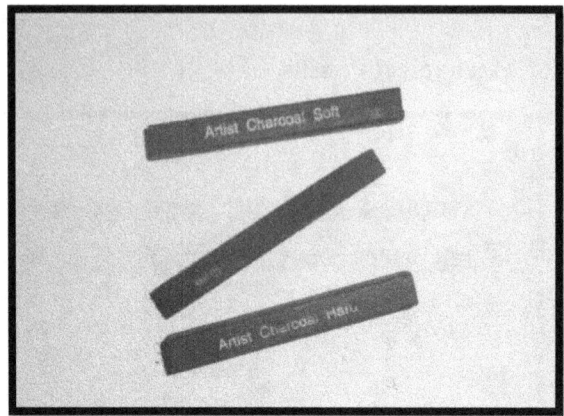

Charcoal bars are rectangular shape charcoal often used by an artist. It has 3 types of textures, the soft, medium and hard. Just like pencils, charcoal comes in a variety of different hardness ratings. The harder the charcoal you use, the lighter the line it will produce on the paper. Some people prefer to use very soft charcoals for their ability to blend or make deeper lines, while others prefer to use a medium rating that lies between hard and soft. But in this tutorial we will use only the soft because it is easy to use and preferable for beginners.

Brush

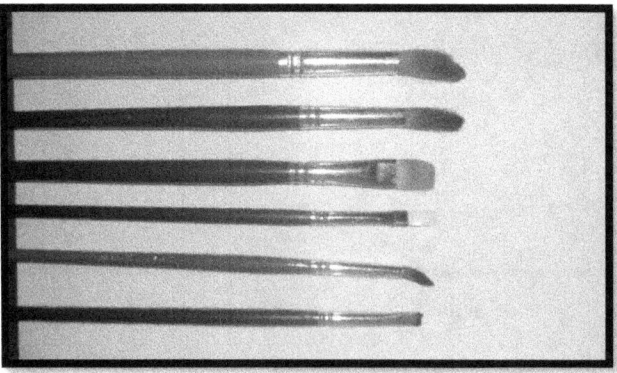

Different types and sizes of brushes are required with this tutorial. You must have a soft bristle brushes to be use in rendering. In other part of this tutorial I will teach you on how to use brush while rendering.

Tortillion or spreader

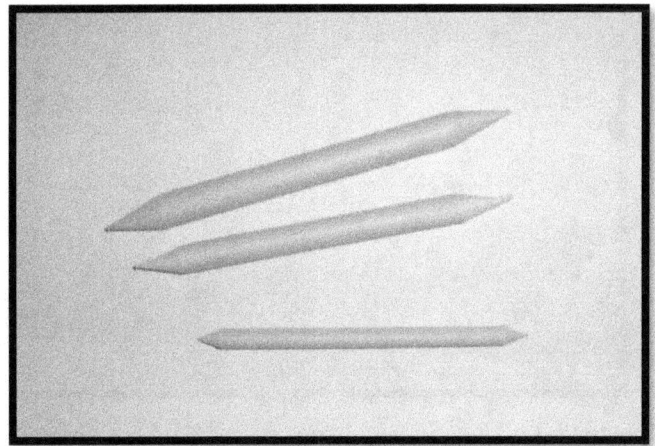

A tortillon or spreader is a cylindrical drawing tool, tapered at the ends and usually made of rolled paper, used by artists to smudge or blend marks made with charcoal, crayon, pencil or other drawing utensils. A blending stump is similar to a tortillon but is longer, more tightly wrapped, and pointed at both ends. Tortillons produce slightly different textures than stumps when blending, and they also are hollow, as opposed to stumps being solid.

Cutter

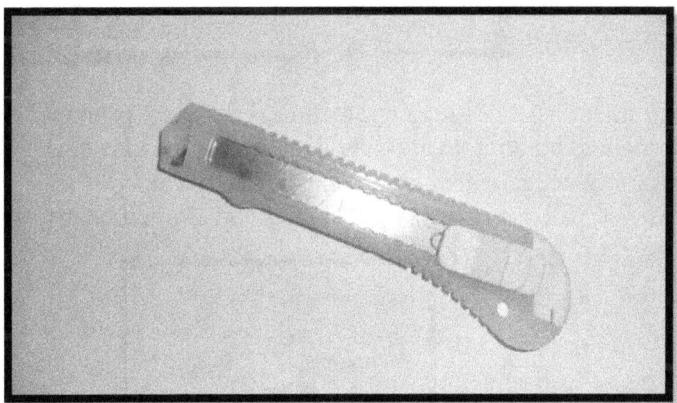

We will use it in sharpening HB pencils and tortillions. Use it properly so that you can avoid cuts or wounds.

Pencil extender or pencil lengthener

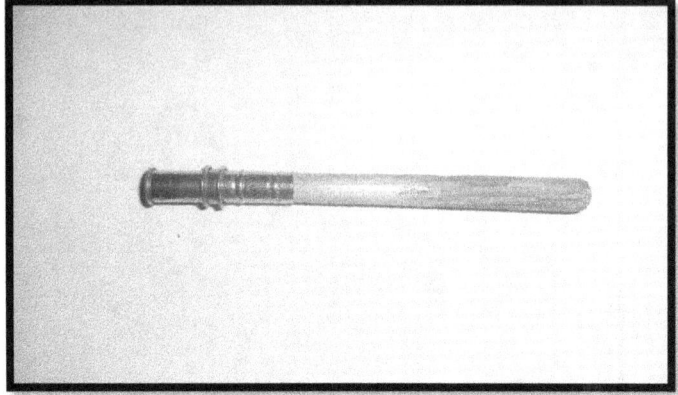

A pencil extender or pencil lengthener is a small instrument made out of metal or wood, allowing to extend small pencils in order to facilitate their use.

Straight edges or ruler

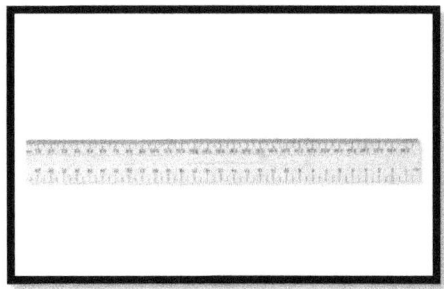

Is an instrument used in geometry, technical drawing, printing as well as engineering and building to measure distances or to rule straight lines. The ruler is a straightedge which may also contain calibrated lines to measure distances. We will use it creating grid lines and straight edges.

Eraser

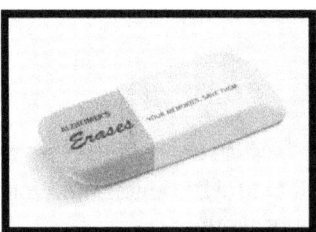

We will use it in erasing mistakes and construction line in sketching.

Kneaded eraser

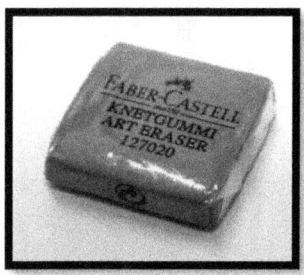

The kneaded eraser, also known as putty rubber, is a tool for artists. It is usually made of a grey or white pliable material (though it can be found in many different colors, ranging from green to blue to hot pink) and resembles putty or gum. It functions by absorbing and "picking up" graphite and charcoal particles. It does not wear away and leave behind eraser residue, thus it lasts much longer than other erasers. Kneaded erasers can be shaped by hand for precision erasing, creating highlights, or performing detailing work. They are commonly used to remove light charcoal or graphite marks and in subtractive drawing techniques. However, they are ill-suited for completely erasing large areas, and may smear or stick if too warm.

Easel

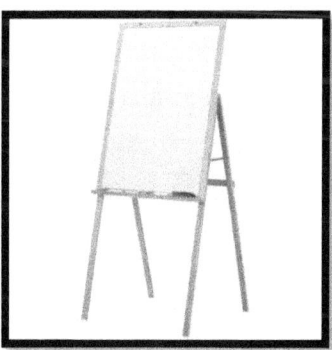

A self-supporting wooden frame for holding an artist's work while it is being painted or drawn. In most instances these can be adjusted to standing or sitting positions. A table easel or a light-weight wooden or metal sketching easel make a practical starting point for the newcomer.

Sketchpad

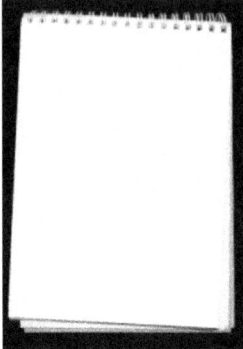

It is preferable for beginners to use sketch pad so that they can able to compile their artworks to see for the improvements.

Cotton

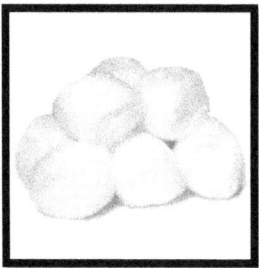

Cotton is a soft, fluffy staple fiber that grows in a boll. The fiber is almost pure cellulose. It is used in spreading charcoal on a large detail of the drawing such as background.

Working Area

Charcoal drawings are fairly dark, particularly when you are learning to smudge, which can make details and highlights difficult to see in shadow. Make sure that your work area is well lit so that you can make out the details easily.

Keep in mind that the best technique when learning to draw with a new medium, such as charcoal, is to work on a vertical surface. You are less likely to drag your arm or the side of your hand through your drawing when working vertically rather than on a horizontal surface. This is particularly helpful when working with charcoal, simply because it smudges and smears so easily that any brushing of your hand across the surface will result in smudging. Using an easel is an ideal way to get the practice you need without unnecessary smudges.

Do's and Don'ts

The images shown below are captured while I paint using acrylic paint. The first image shows that the canvas board was mounted in an easel and the second one on the other hand, was put on the top of the table which is not necessarily.

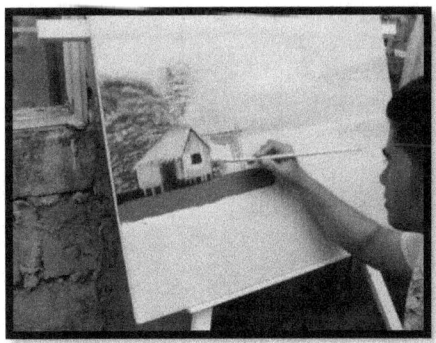
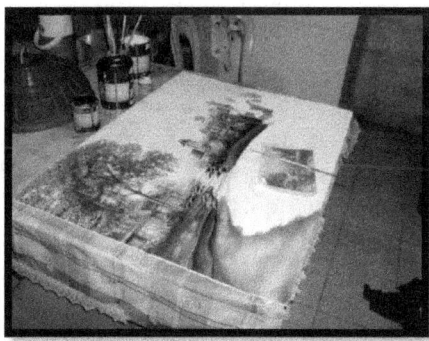

Do   Don't

Still Life

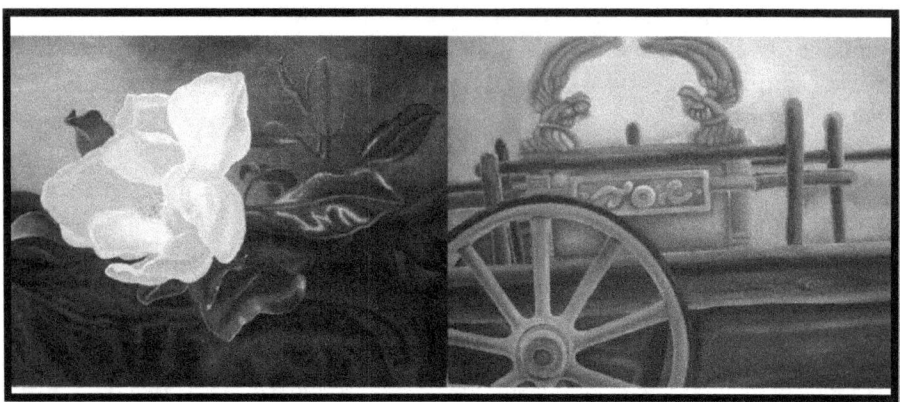

A still life is a work of art depicting mostly inanimate subject matter, typically commonplace objects which may be either natural or man-made. With origins in the Middle Ages and Ancient Graeco-Roman art, still-life painting emerged as a distinct genre and professional specialization in Western painting by the late 16th century, and has remained significant since then. Still life gives the artist more freedom in the arrangement of elements within a composition than do paintings of other types of subjects such as landscape or portraiture.

I learned still life when I was in high school. My father taught me on how to do this kind of craft. At first, it was a quiet difficult for me but it doesn't mean that I will give up. That's why I study it, practice well and research about still life drawing. I used a simple pencil that time and it is strangely awesome for me to do this kind of art. I draw a simple circular shape and render it using the pencil and my index finger and cotton. After a year I started to use charcoal pencil and charcoal bars as my medium in doing still life.

Values of Shade

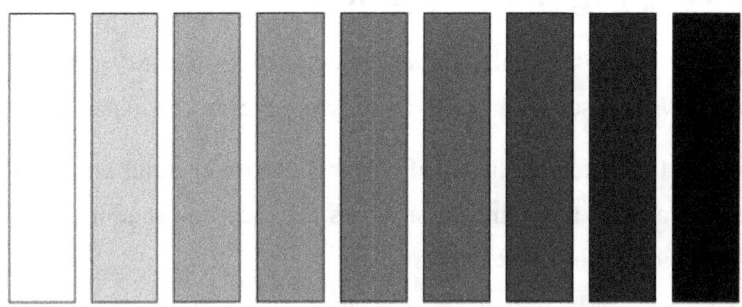

Highlight (white)   **Shadow** (black)

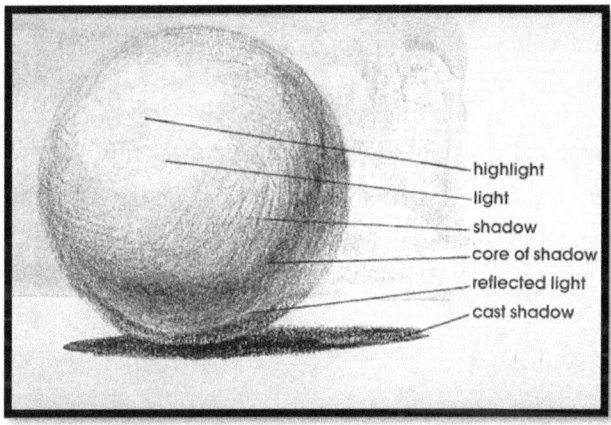

highlight
light
shadow
core of shadow
reflected light
cast shadow

Light source: The direction from which a dominant light originates. The placement of this light source affects every aspect of a drawing.

Shadows: The areas on an object that receive little or no light.

Cast shadow: The dark area on an adjacent surface where the light is blocked by the solid object.

The shadows on the object (dark values)

The brightest areas (the highlights)

The light values (areas closer to the light source or not in shadow)

The cast shadow (the darkest values)

Drawing Light and Shadows

Light and shadows visually define objects. Before you can draw the light and shadows you see, you need to train your eyes to see like an artist.

Values are the different shades of gray between white and black. Artists use values to translate the light and shadows they see into shading, thus creating the illusion of a third dimension.

Hatching and crosshatching are simple and fun techniques for drawing shading.

A full range of values is the basic ingredient for shading. When you can draw lots of different values, you can begin to add shading, and therefore depth, to your drawings.

With shading, the magical illusion of three-dimensional reality appears on your drawing paper. Exercise 1 demonstrates how to take a simple line drawing of a circle and add shading to transform it into a still life drawing.

Exercise 1: Sphere

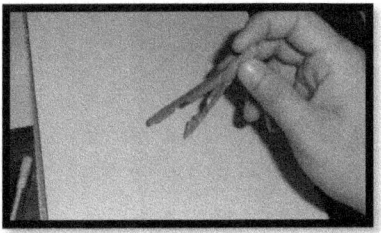 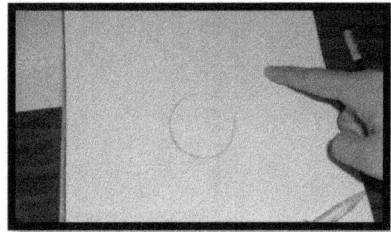

1. Draw a circle or a sphere using your compass.

2. Point out where your light source coming from, often it is from the top like my index finger pointing out.

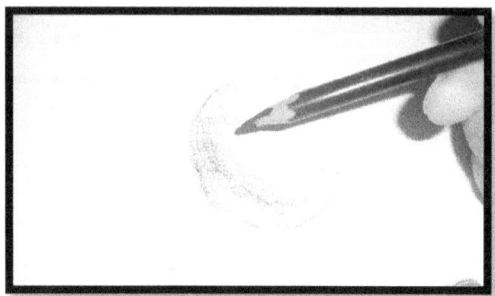

3. Now start to render the surface of the circle using your charcoal pencil. Make sure that you must follow the shape or stroke of the circle.

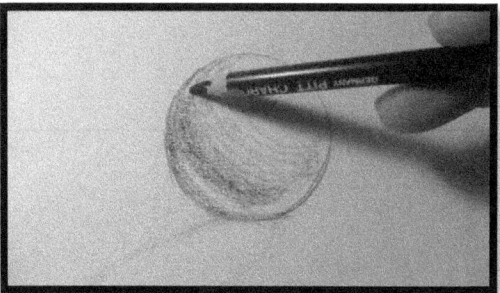

4. Suppose to be the light source is coming from the right top therefore the shadow must be in the lower left of the circle.

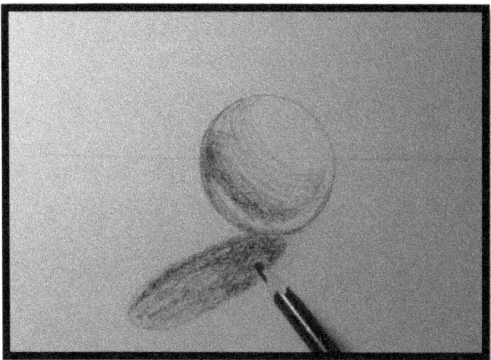

5. Draw the cast shadow under the circle and shade it.

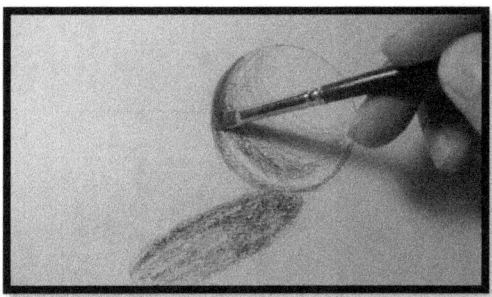

6. Use the small soft brush to spread the charcoal on the surface of the paper to make it smooth.

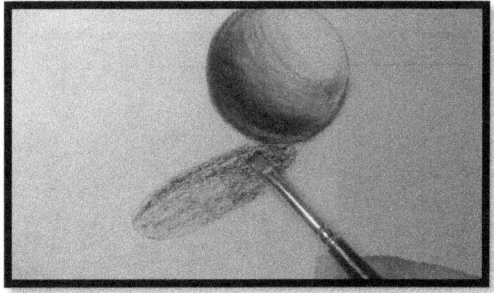

7. Spread thoroughly so that it will blend.

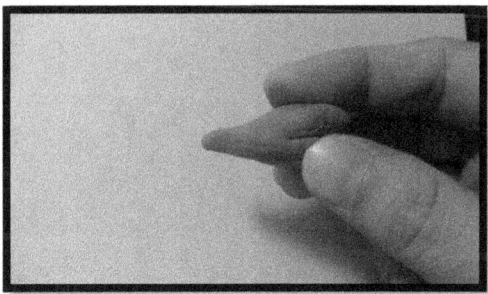

8. Get a small amount of your kneaded eraser and mold it with a pointed tip.

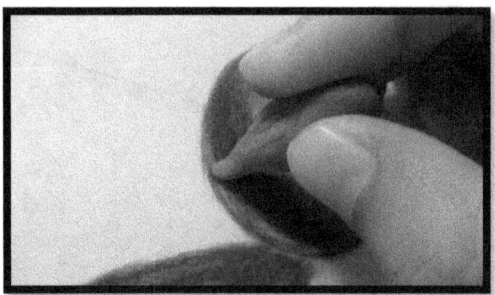

9. Erase the lower surface of the circle to make its reflected light visible.

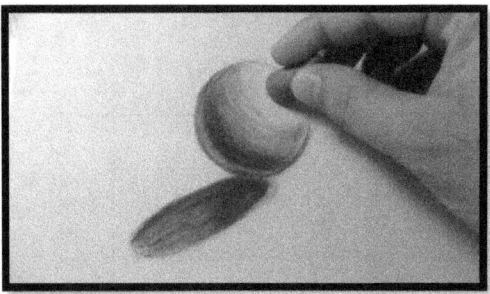

10. Highlight the portion of the object that hits the source of light.

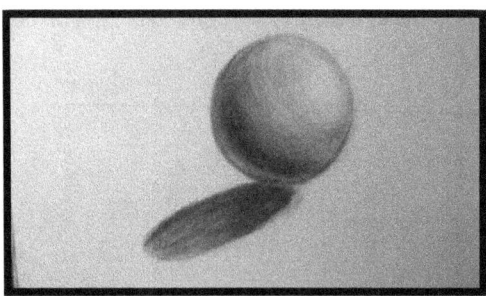

11. This is the result of the light and shadow of a sphere. Moving on to still life.

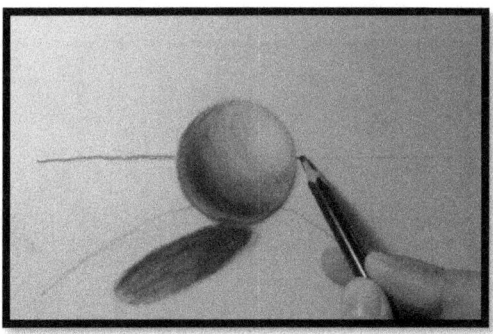

12. Now draw a horizontal line in the middle part of the circle and draw an arc like what you see in the illustration.

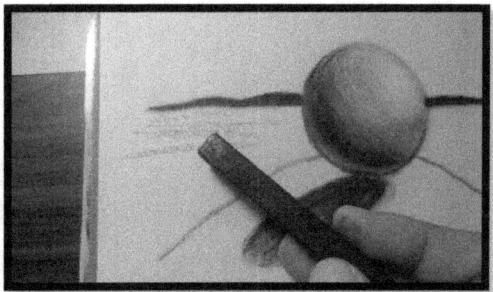

13. Using your soft charcoal bar, draw a mountain in the horizontal line that will serve as the background. And shade the spaces between the arc and the horizontal line.

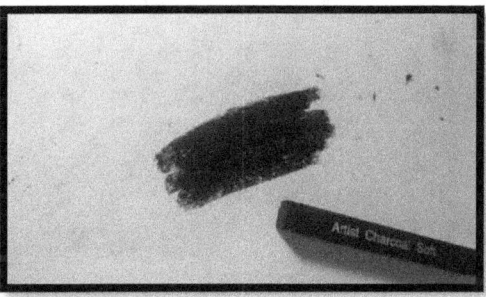

14. Get an extra paper and scratch your charcoal bar to produce a powdered charcoal.

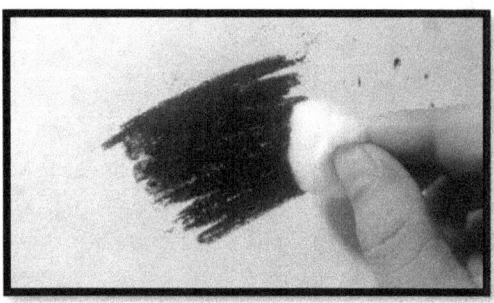

15. Use cotton ball for application.

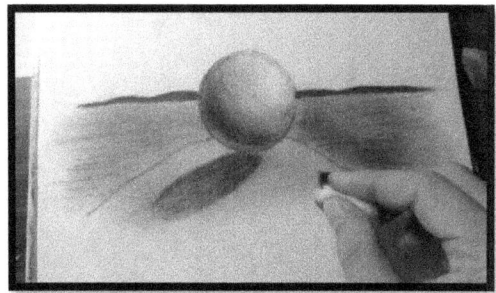

16. Apply the charcoal powder in the drawing to make it blend.

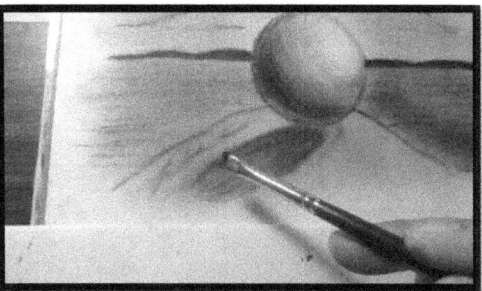

17. Use your brush and produce some details on the background and to the ground.

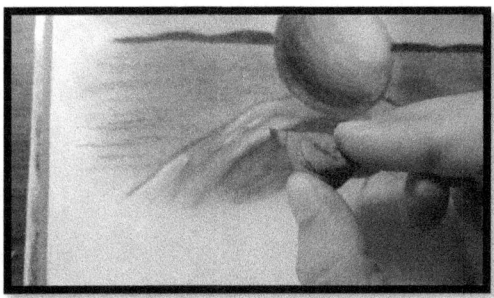

18. Put some detail by using the kneaded eraser and erase the edges as seen in the illustration.

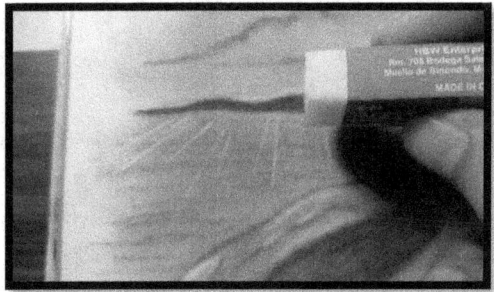

19. Draw lines towards the mountain to make it looks like it is far away.

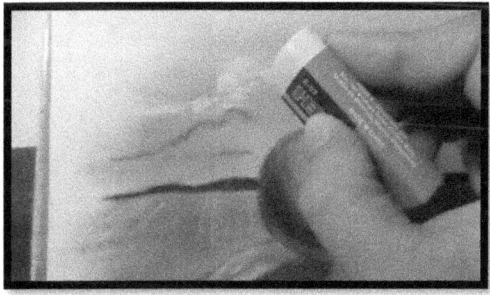

20. Put some clouds using your eraser. And then erase the sun or the light source completely.

It goes like this.

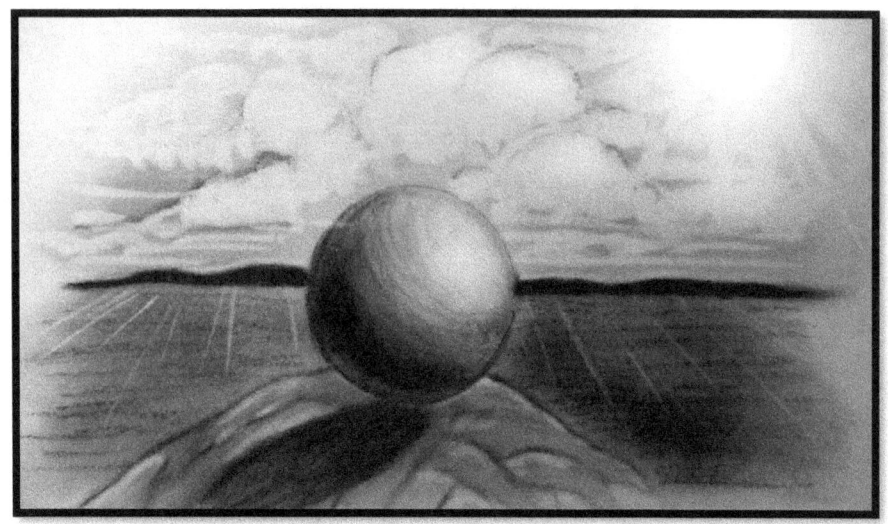

Still Life of a Sphere

Exercise 2: Metal Pot

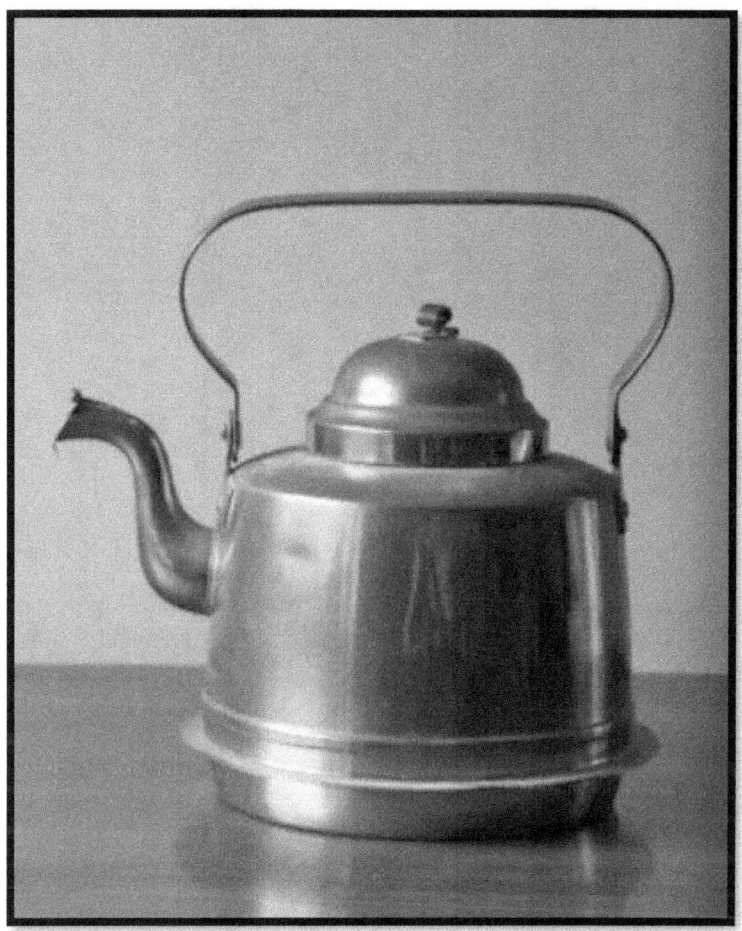

 Often beginner artist tend to draw various types of textures. In this case we will draw a metal pot with a metallic and smooth texture. I always encourage my classmates and co-artists to try a black and white drawing. As we take the first exercise, we have the same procedure but it is more difficult by this time. Prepare your materials and get ready to learn.

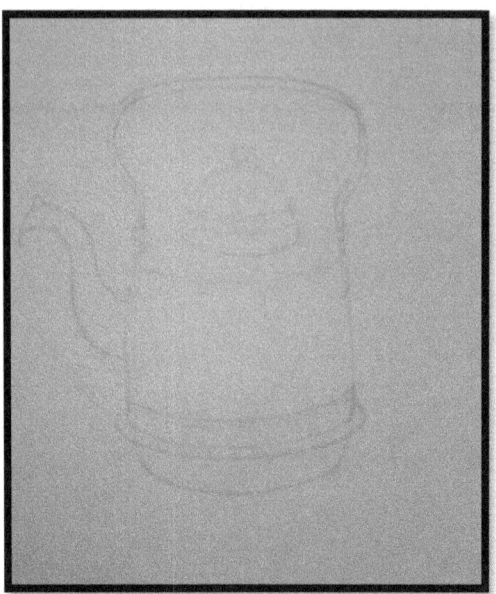

1. First, you must sketch the model using your HB pencil. When you have made your sketch turn it upside down and look at it before you start to render it with charcoal. Any errors will show up and can be corrected.

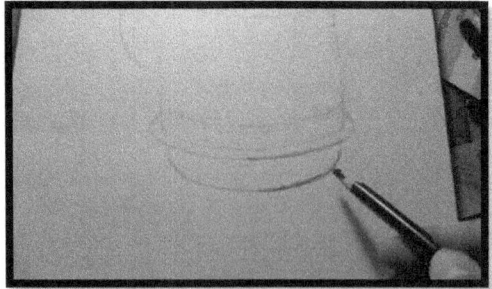

2. Find the area which you will start to render. Using the charcoal pencil highlight the base outline of the pot.

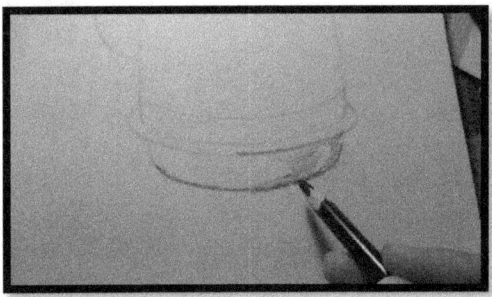

3. Shade it thoroughly with the image values. Make sure that you are following its stroke.

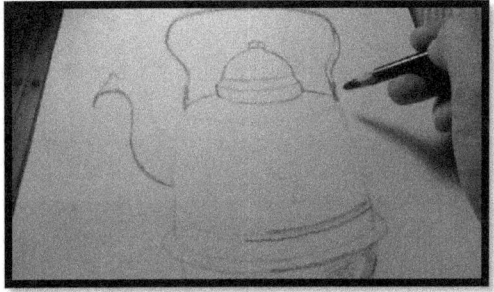

4. Also highlight its handle. Don't forget to look at your reference so that you can see the difference.

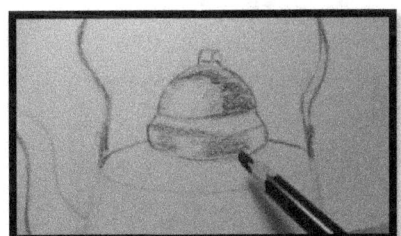 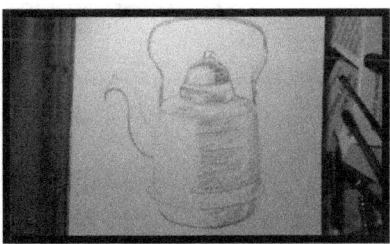

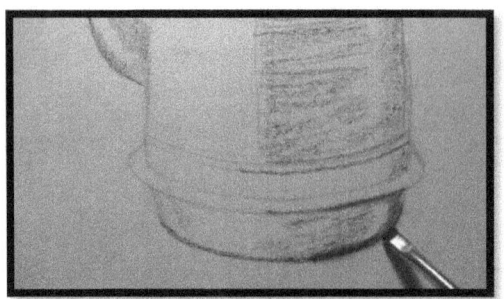

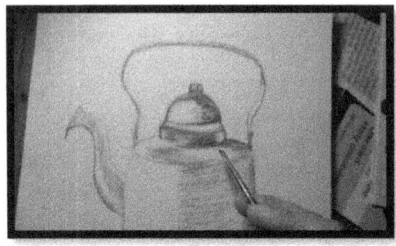
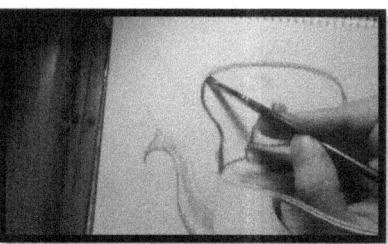

5. Just spread the charcoal thoroughly to your object. You must start to the darkest portion then to light portion.

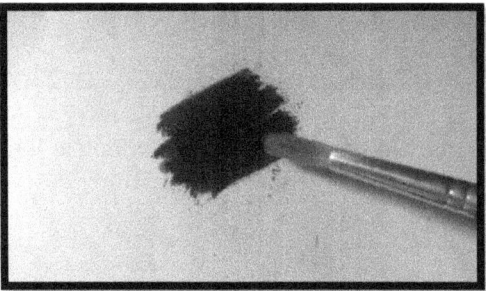

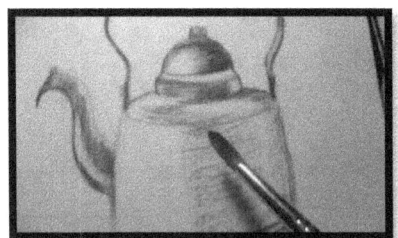
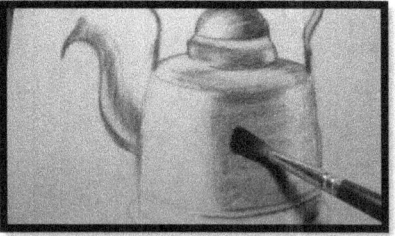

6. Scratch your compressed charcoal into the paper to produce powdered charcoal then apply it using your brush.

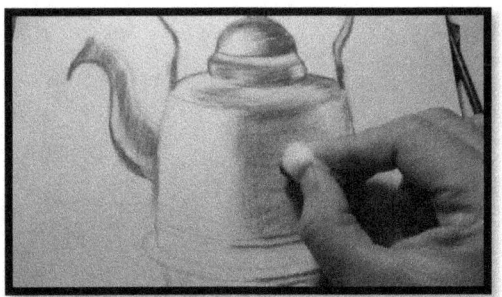

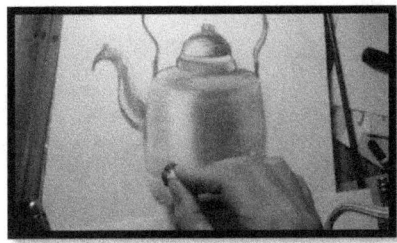
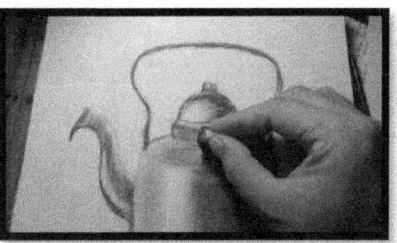

7. Then use cotton to make it smooth. The harder the shading the better results. Use a clean, dry, soft cloth or duster and vigorously dust the surface of the picture. The loose, smudgy charcoal is removed by the duster leaving you with a faint, non-smudgy drawing ready to be shaded.

8. Cut a little portion of your eraser then place it on the pencil extender.

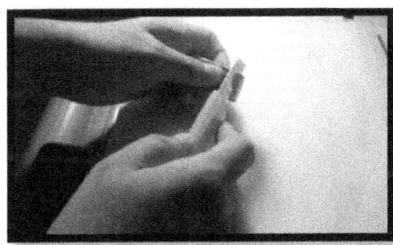
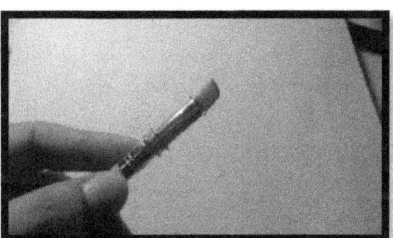

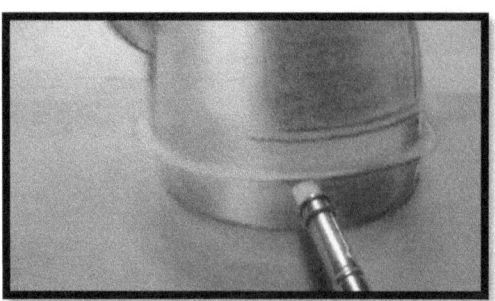

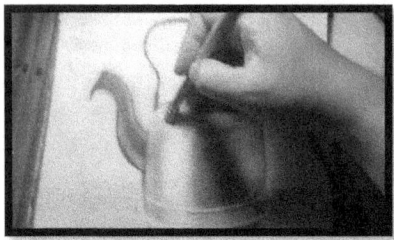
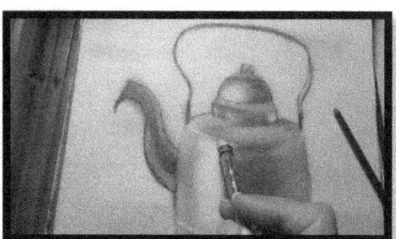

9. Highlight the light portion using this tool.

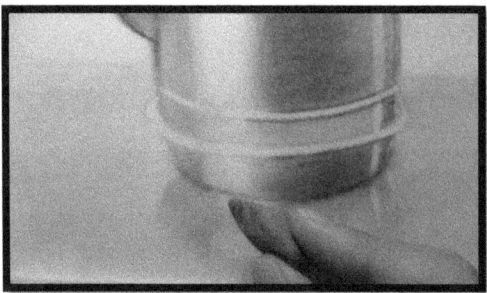

10. Use your kneaded eraser to create the reflection of the light in the pot. As you can see in the illustration it looks like it has a glossy surface in the base. Finalize it.

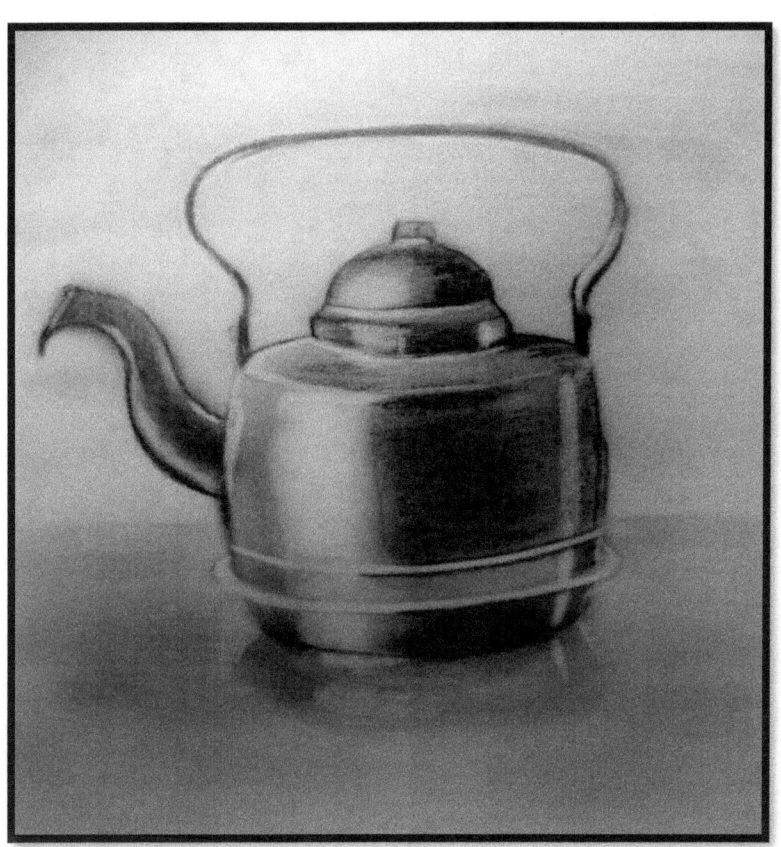

The Metal Pot

Exercise 3: Fruits

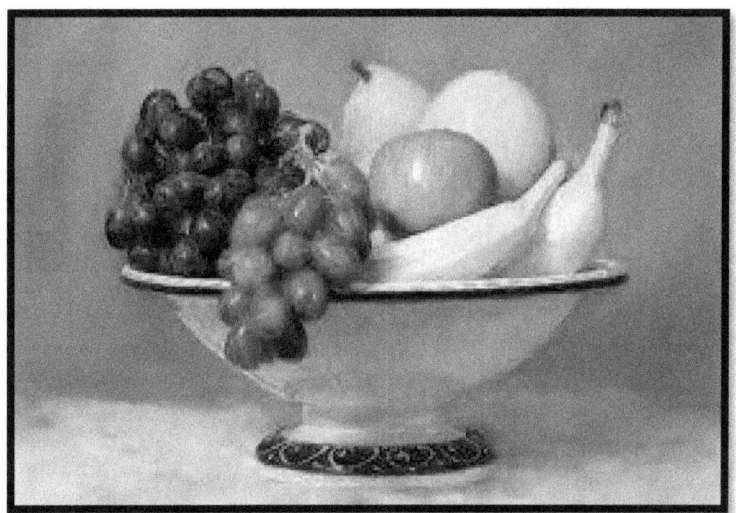

There are lots of interesting and exciting subjects all around us. This group of fruits is probably a sample of a perfect subject to be a reference. You can also create your own subject in actual or they called it on-the-spot sketching. Just place some objects such as fruits, kitchenware or anything that can be seen inside the house and put it on the top of your table. You can also decide what is the good angle.

1. Sketch the object into your sketch pad.

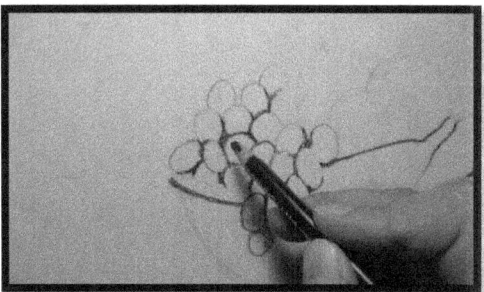

2. Darken the dark portion using your charcoal pencil. Highlight the outline of your object.

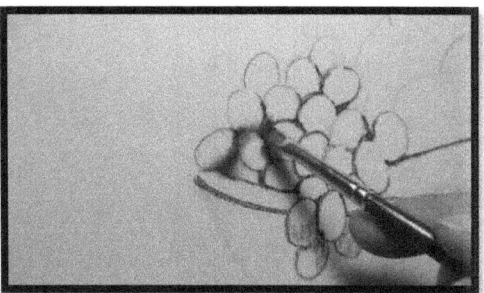

3. Spread the charcoal using brush to make it blend.

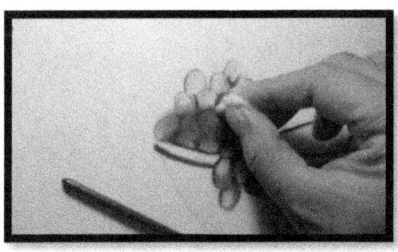 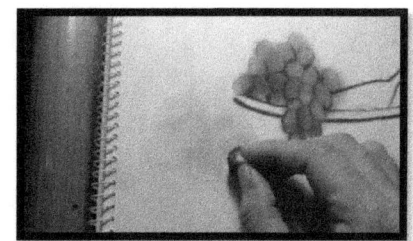

4. Use the cotton to spread the charcoal from the object to the background.

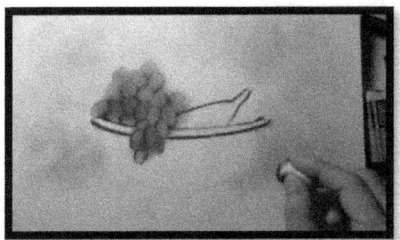 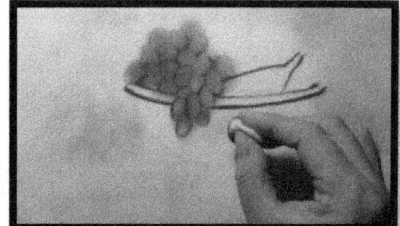

5. Spread thoroughly until it blend.

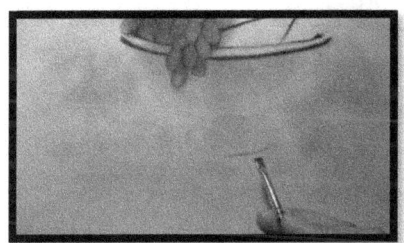 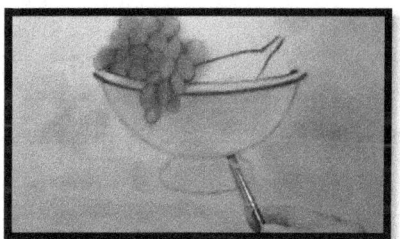

6. Use the brush to detail the outline of the object. Make sure it will not too dark.

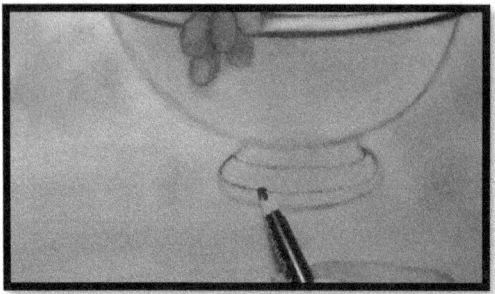

7. Use your charcoal pencil to highlight the details with dark values.

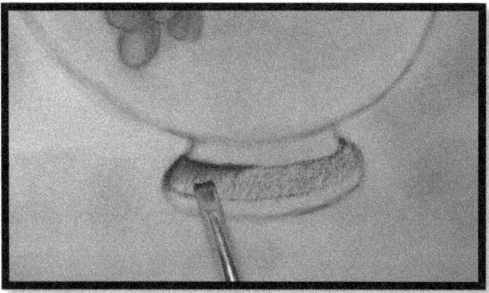

8. Spread the dark portion using your brush.

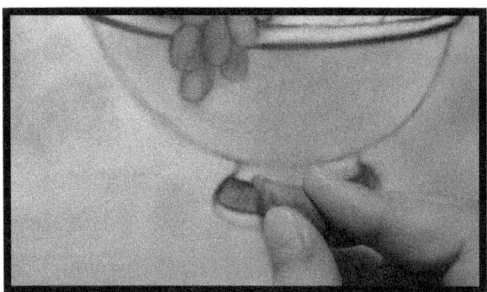

9. Highlight the light portion using kneaded eraser. But before that you should know where the light source is coming from.

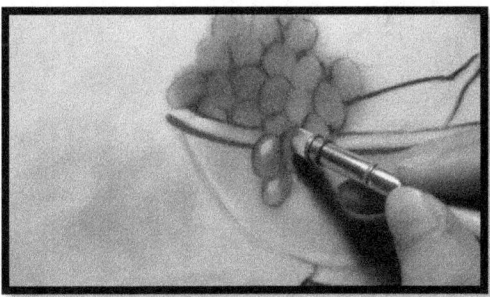

10. Using your eraser create catch light to your grapes so that it will looks like it has a source of light coming from the front.

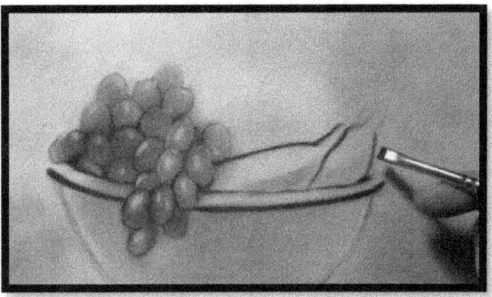

11. Just continue the procedure above. And then proceed to the details of banana. The edges should be fine using your brush.

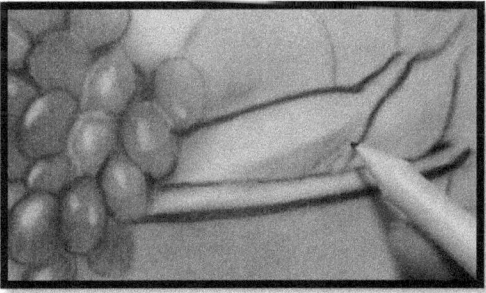

12. And also use your tortillion or spreader to detail the edges and the dirt of banana. Like what you see in the illustration.

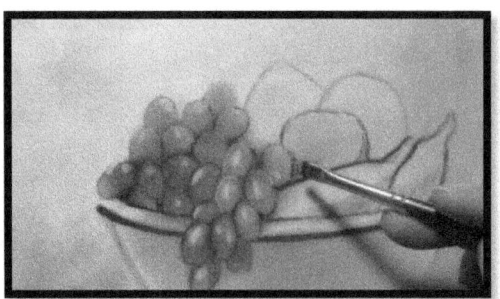

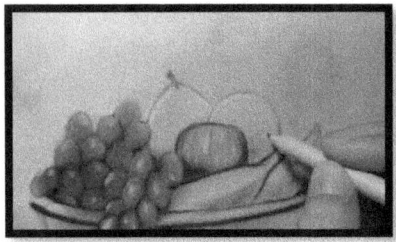
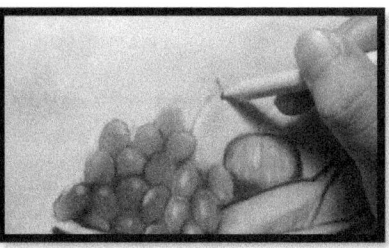

13. The same procedure, work out in all the details of the fruits. But don't overwork.

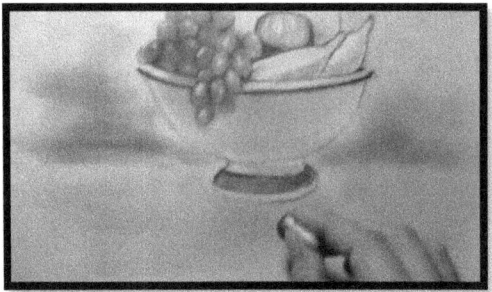

14. Use the cotton to shade the background and the base. Then finalize it.

Fruits

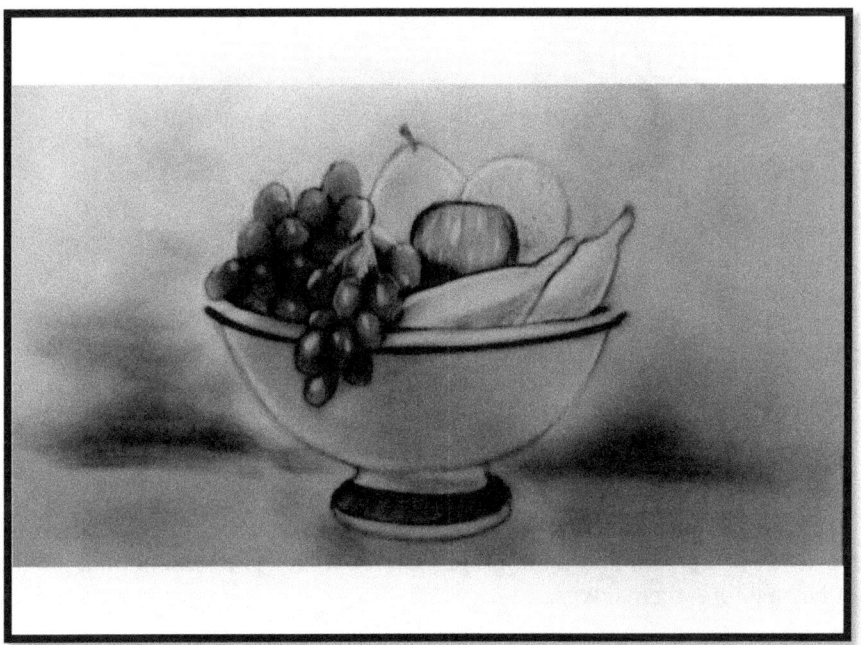

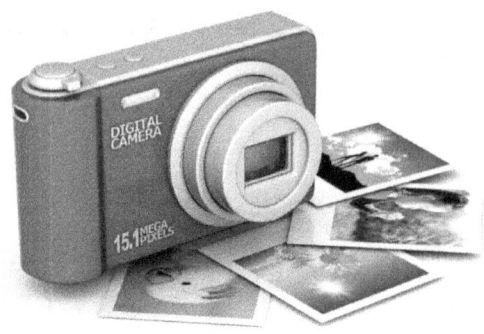

Drawing from Photographs

Some artist say never copy from photographs, others say it is quite alright to do so. I am often asked who is right. A camera can be an invaluable tool for an artist. The camera and photographs can be a means to an end, but should not be an end in themselves.

When I go out sketching I usually take my camera with me. A combination of sketches with the back-up reference of photographs provide all that is needed to produce one or more drawings in the work area. Sometimes if outdoors, or on holiday with family and friends, I see a subject I would love to draw but there is not even time to make a sketch. The camera provides a quick snapshot of the subject for later use.

If a person is housebound, photographs can provide a regular source of material to work from. Do not however copy the photograph slavishly. Let your own style and interpretation of the subject come through in the drawing.

You will often find a subject within a subject. Below I show a photograph of a pair of shoes. If you don't have a camera, you can use your mobile phone or other gadget with camera. Make sure that you're captured photos are clear so that you can easily copy it. So get your camera and let's start.

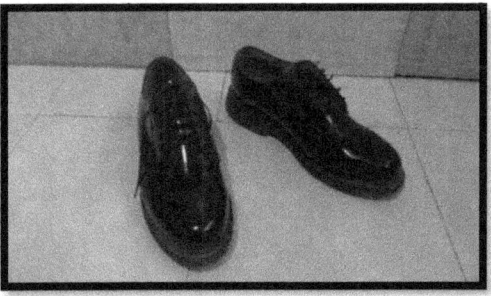

1. First, you must capture a photo using your camera. All that you actually see are all have potential to be your subject, but choose a simple object.

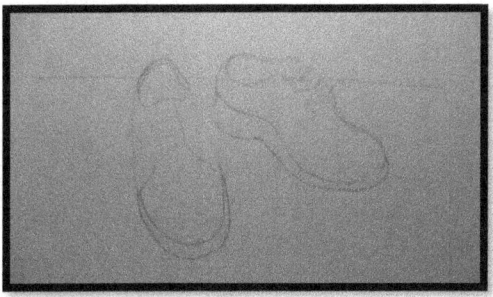

2. Use your charcoal pencil and firmly draw out the object. The line should look black but will easily smudge. As I mentioned above, do not slavishly copy the photograph. That's why I only apply a rough sketch. Create your own style and be creative.

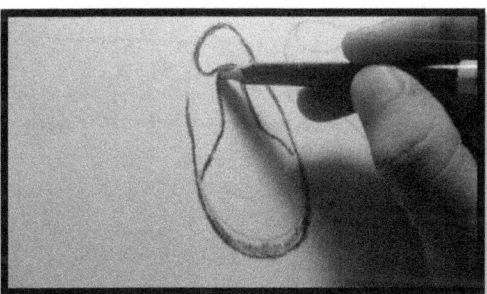

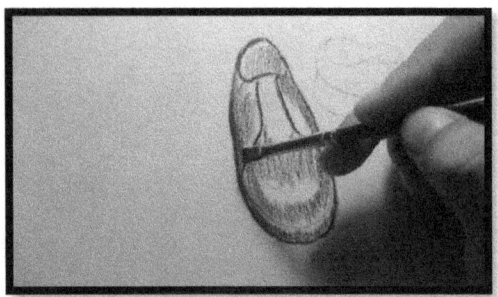

3. Apply the procedure we do in our previous exercises.

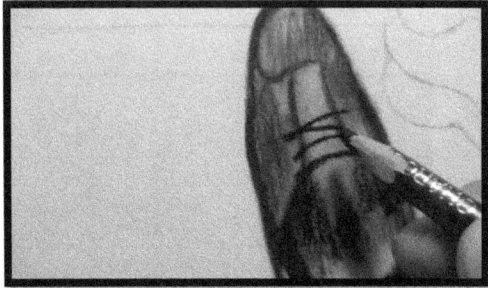

4. Firmly draw the shoe tie with your charcoal pencil.

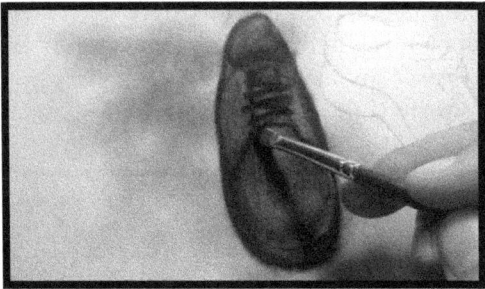

5. Spread the charcoal using soft cotton and brush. Do the same thing in the background.

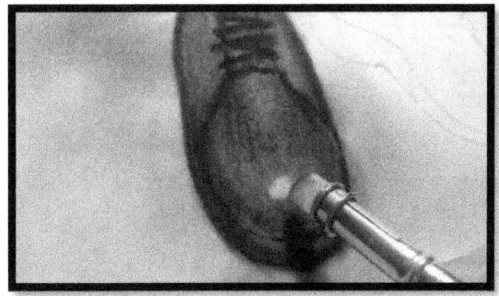

6. Now highlight the catch light using your eraser to make it looks real.

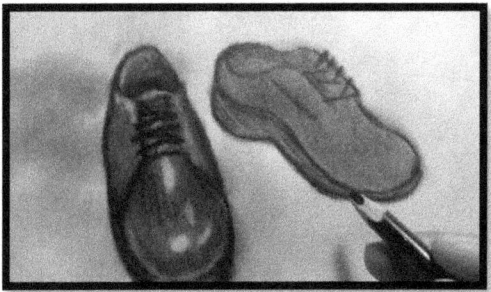

7. Just continue the same procedure and proceed to the other shoe.

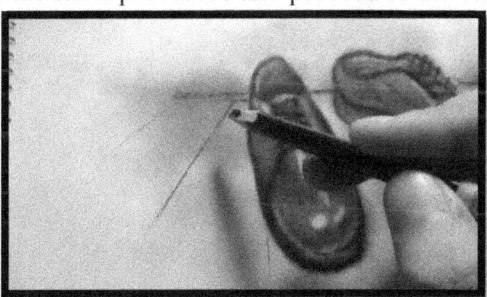

8. After you've done doing the same procedure. Draw some lines what you see in the illustration. Just be creative and do not limit your creativity. Finalize your details.

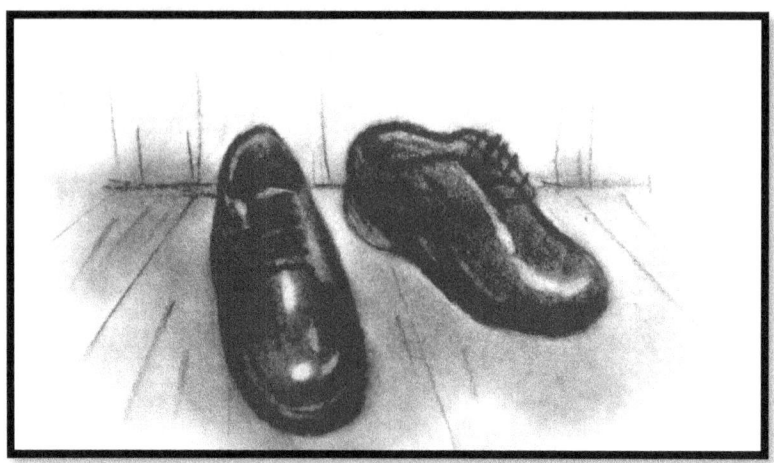

Tips to remember:

When you start a charcoal drawing, it's best to work vertically on an easel or drawing horse. This allows the charcoal dust to fall away, and lets you see the whole drawing without any distortion or foreshortening like you might see if working on a flat surface. Make sure to secure your paper or sketchpad to a rigid surface before you begin, such as a drawing board with clips, or you will be spending a lot of time holding your drawing still with one hand while drawing with the other.

Sometimes the strokes and marks of compressed charcoal are desirable, and sometimes they aren't. With cotton you can start smoothing and blending some of your values to get more even tones, as well as extend your marks a bit further without directly applying charcoal.

 To create crisp hard-lined highlights and value shapes, use quick assertive strokes with your eraser. Be careful not to keep working over the area or it could smudge!

Don't overwork! Use your best judgment to determine when your drawing is finished. One of the best qualities of charcoal is how it allows you to leave some parts of a drawing unrefined and sketchy while developing other areas more fully. Think about where you'd like to keep your drawing loose and gestural, and where you want it more "finished."

Now, go out and explore the possibilities of charcoal drawing! Just remember to wash your hands afterwards. It can get a bit messy! Keep on practicing more. Thank you for reading this e-book.

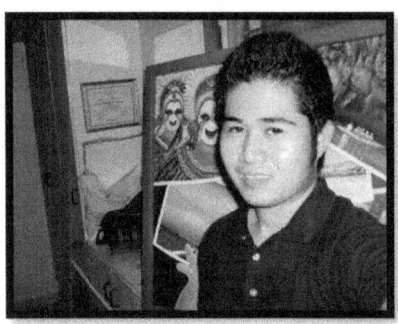

Author Bio

Mark Anthony Lingat

An inborn Artist and Draftsman, Experience in painting and drawing for more than 10 years. He is also a sand artist performing in different events. He lives in Pampanga, Philippines.

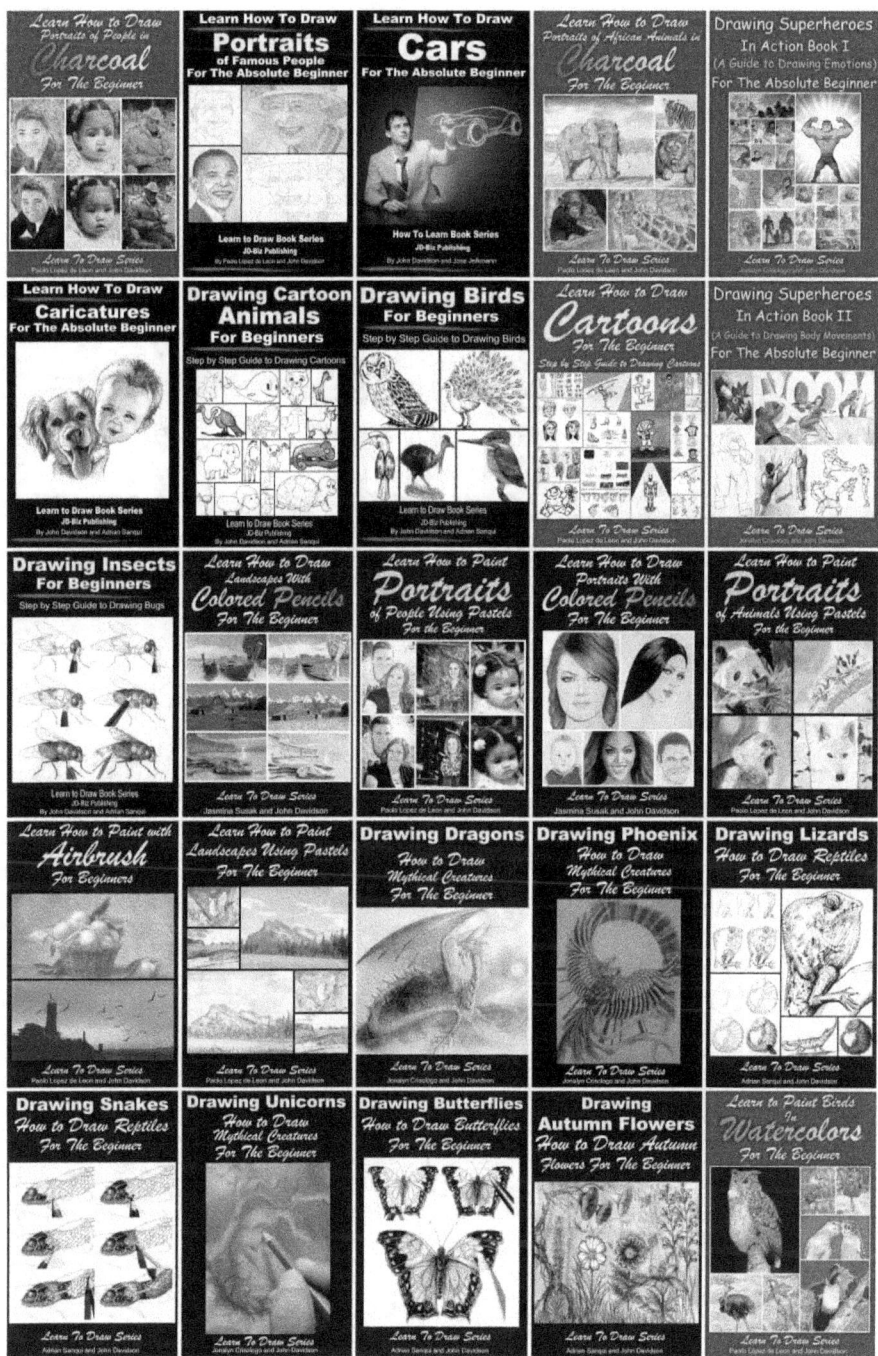

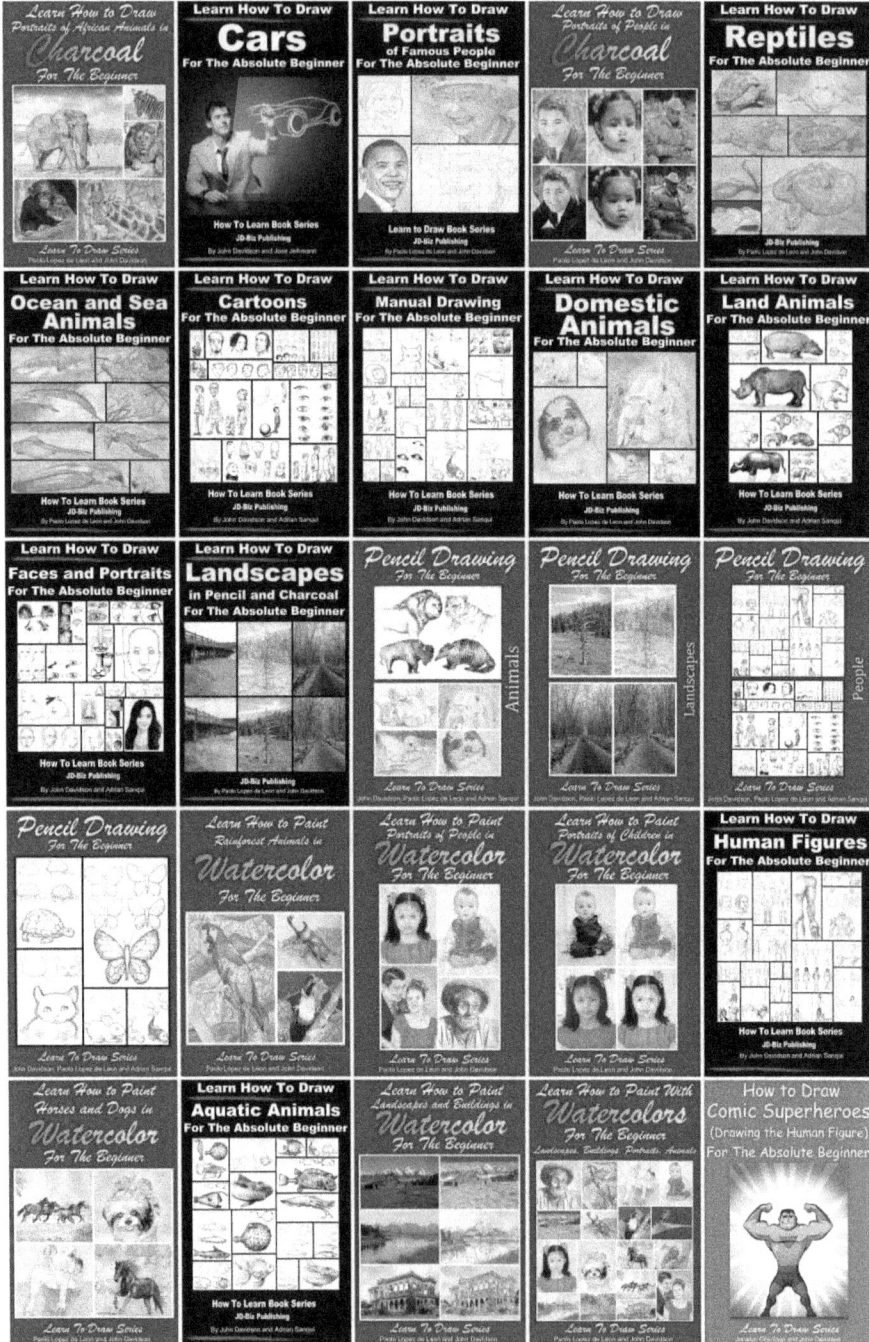

Publisher

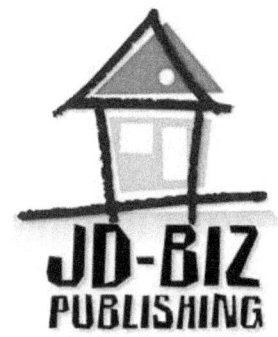

JD-Biz Corp

P O Box 374

Mendon, Utah 84325

http://www.jd-biz.com/

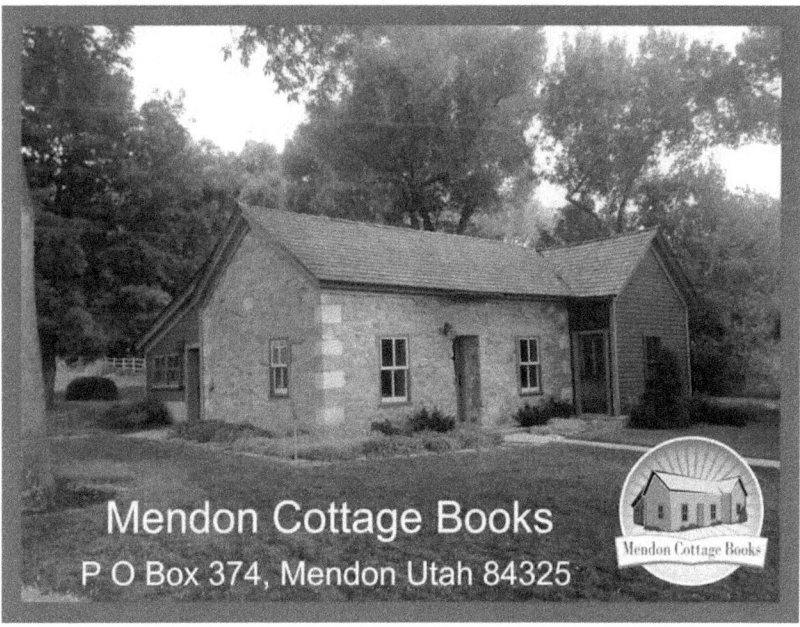

Mendon Cottage Books
P O Box 374, Mendon Utah 84325

Bonus Book

Learn How to Draw Portraits of

African Animals in Charcoal

For the Beginner

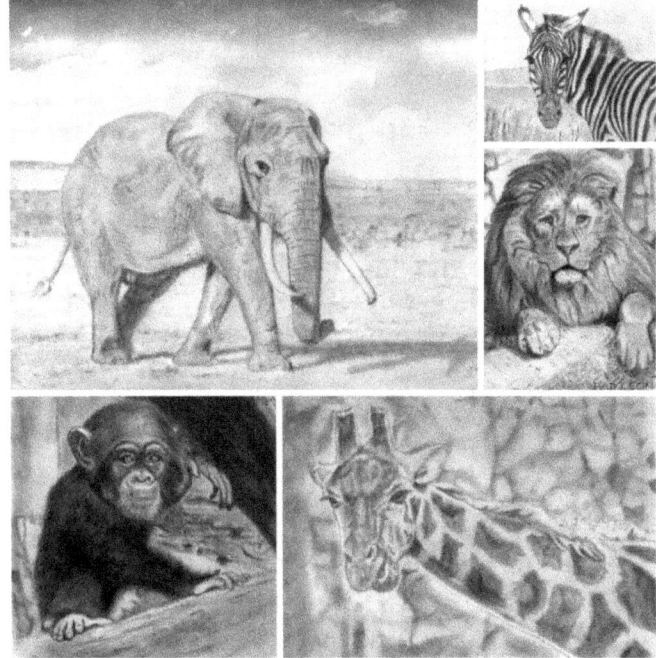

Paolo Lopez de Leon
And
John Davidson

Learn to Draw
Book Series

JD- Biz Publishing

Learn How to Draw Books for the Absolute Beginner

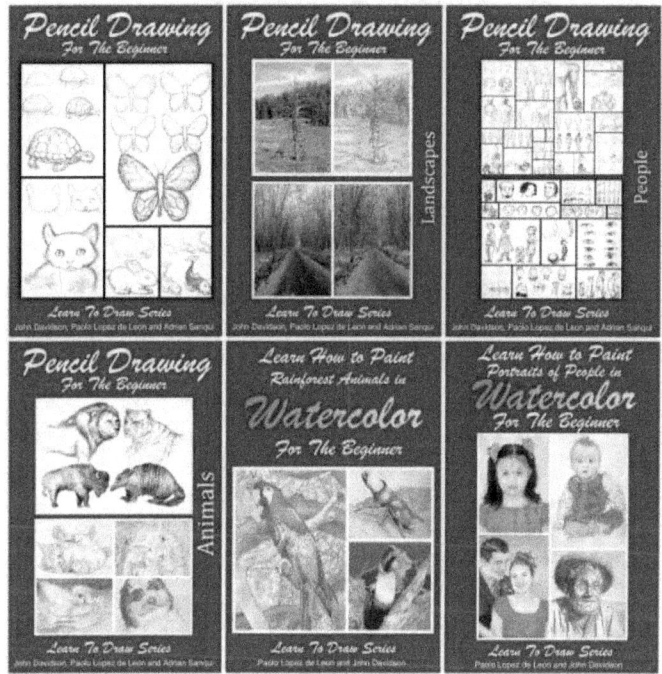

TABLE OF CONTENTS

Introduction:
Materials
Shaving the Charcoal
Rendering Using Charcoal
Application
Drawing an Outline
Grid System
Tracing Table or Light Table / Flexi-glass with Bendable Lamp
Tips to Remember
Exercises
Zebra
Giraffe
Elephant
Baby Chimp
Lion
Author Bio

Introduction:

Ever wonder how artist draw Portrait of an African animal, especially if they used Charcoal as there medium. Also have you also try to draw and render them even with your pencil and after that you're not happy of what you see with the result, and no matter how you try even with a slight improvement, still it's not convincing enough to look like your subject. And you're frustrated with this as if you're going to give up, well this scenario can happen to anyone, including me when I was learning to draw animals, but now you're very fortunate, because I will teach you how to draw African Animal Portraits using Charcoal.

Anyone in any age can learn this, for beginners and also artist who want to enhance their artistic skills in the world of Charcoal. As you know Charcoal evokes a different feeling when compared to other media, even as a viewer you will feel the depth of any Charcoal works in front of you, so that's amazing. And we will be drawing and rendering African animals, to add the feeling of excitement, as if we're having a tour in Safari or Zoo.

You will learn the right materials for our Charcoal works, basics, and techniques. So give your time and dedication, set time to read this book and most of all practice by doing the exercises, follow my step-by-step instructions and in no time you will be Animal portrait Artist. So let's begin the journey and have fun with Charcoal.

Materials

Mechanical Pencils

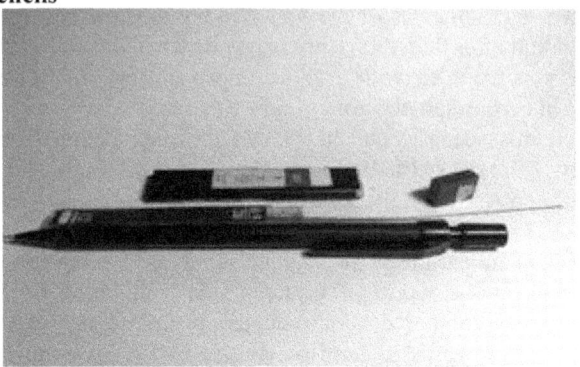

Like Pencils the lead is also made of Graphite, Good for details, come in handy especially for tight areas, the difference is it doesn't need a sharpener if the lead breaks, just press the cap on the end of the pencil and it's good to go, it comes in different sizes: 0.2mm to 5.6mm, for our drawing 0.5 will just be suffice.

Charcoal

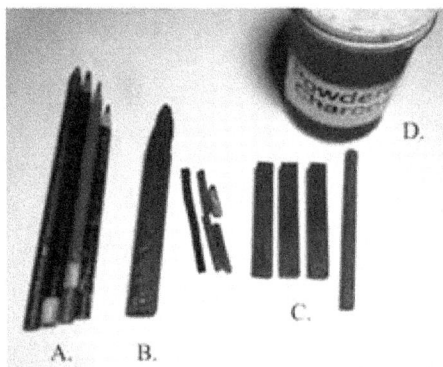

Said to be the oldest medium for drawing, use by Art Masters all over the world, and when smudge can create wonderful effects.

- A. Charcoal pencils-Comes in different range: Hard, Medium and Soft, good for giving details in any charcoal work.
- B. Vine Charcoal- They also comes in different range and also sizes, you can apply it directly or shave it with your cutter and use the accumulated dust in your working paper.
- C. Compress Charcoals- The same as other charcoal, with different range and in shapes, available in bar or cylindrical shape, they have more darker tone and can easily adhere to any drawing paper.

D. Powder Charcoal-They comes in cans or plastic bottles, very fine and useful for any charcoal work specially for toning, can also be use for transferring your drawing or outlines to working paper.

Brushes

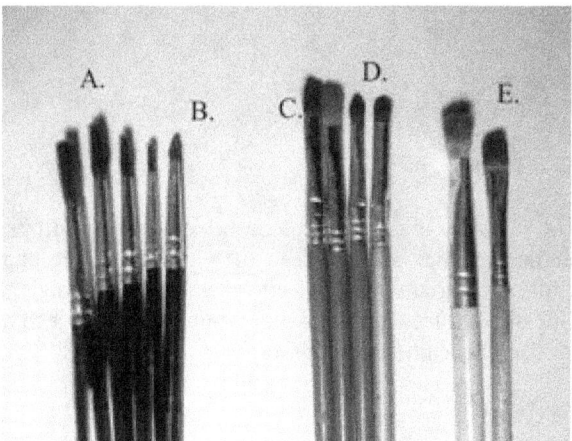

They come in natural and synthetic, natural brush was taken from animal hair: squirrel, weasel, Pony and other land mammals. While synthetic brush is made of synthetic fibers like Nylon. Advantage of synthetic brush includes, less deterioration in terms of time and easy to clean.

For our works, we're going to use the following:
A. Rounded Nylon Brush- Use when applying a light pressure of Charcoal tone that has soft edges. Choose a fine kind of this brush and since sizes varies depending to the manufacturers, just get a brush that have these following width in my case it .2cm width-that would be my small brush, for my med-size brush it measure .3cm, and for the large one it's almost.5cm. You can add another range of brush to have variety of sizes. I seen other artist uses sizes with even numbers-0,2,4,6,8,10 and 12, so see what works for you.
B. Flat Nylon Brush- Use it to apply darker tone and hard edges, usually use when doing aggressive strokes. For the sizes you can use the even numbers to get different kinds of range. In my case, I used no.4 flat Nylon brush mostly on my works.
C. Large Flat Nylon Brush (long handle) - Used for areas that need dark tones.
D. Old Used Brushes- Used as scrubbers, when we need to achieve specific dark tones so that the charcoal dust will adhere to the working paper. Use aggressive strokes and be careful not to ruin the painting surface.
E. Long Soft Hair or Synthetic brush- Use to cover large dust tones in large areas, like hair on the head.

Erasers

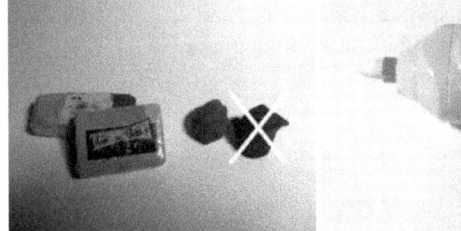 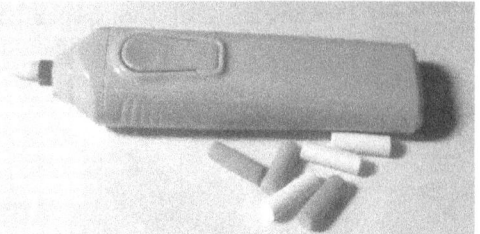

- **Kneaded Eraser**

This is like a clay or putty eraser, which can be mold to any difference shape and thickness, depending to your needs, it can lift Graphite in the paper without any damage, good for tight areas, can lighten areas in your drawing, and used for making highlights in your drawings to make it more realistic. Need to be replaced if it is already dark due to accumulation of Graphite.

- **Vinyl Eraser**

This kind of eraser does not smudge the surface of the paper; it can erase hard and tough areas totally especially for large areas, and does not harden.
There are other types of Erasers like Pink Eraser, Typewriter Erasers and Peel-Off type Eraser, you can also use those, as it depends on the availability of the materials in your area, feel free to experiment what works best for you.

- **Electric Eraser**

It's a battery operated eraser, used by professional's artist, some models comes with soft and abrasive eraser, use not just for erasing tough areas, but can also create highlights and various effects.

Sharpener

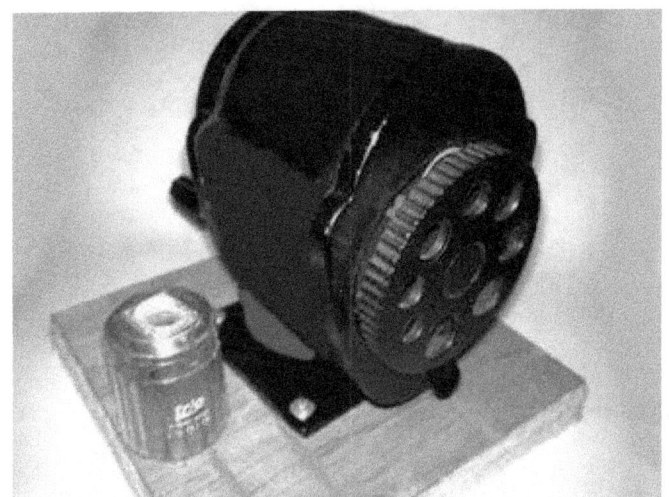

There is manual Sharpener, Wall-Mounted Sharpener and Electric Pencil Sharpener, Any type of Pencil sharpener will do, just make sure that it is safe to use. Use to sharpen the Pencil and Charcoal Pencil.

Cutter

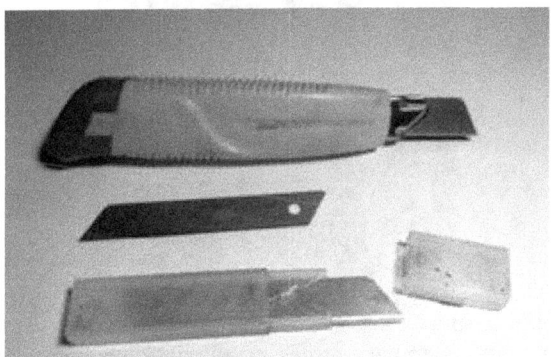

Use to shave the Charcoal and use the accumulated dust on your work. Can be use to sharpen your pencil and Charcoal pencil also, but make sure to be careful not to cut yourself.

Sandpaper

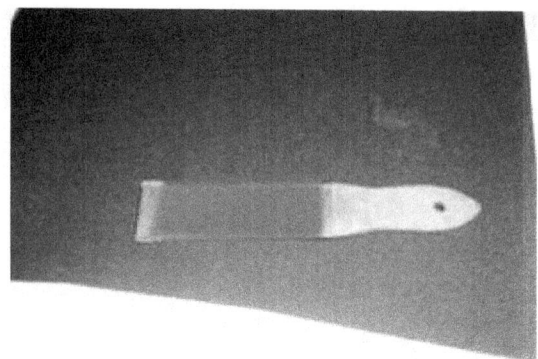

Can be use to sharpen your Pencils and Charcoal. Use 220 grit and cut it to small pieces that you can use. In my case, I place a piece in my old Sandpaper Pencil Pointer.

Spray Fixative

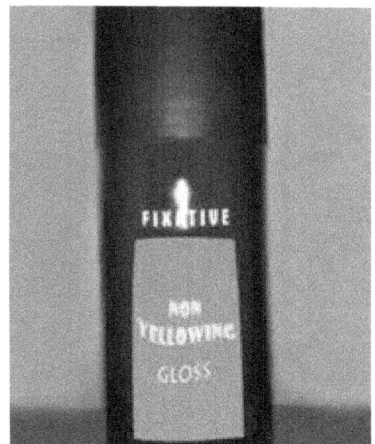

These are available in spray cans, it will make you're drawing fix to the paper, so that it will not smudge and to have professional looks, they comes in Matte or Gloss Finish, better to choose a trusted brand and a non-yellowing.

Smudge Sticks or Tortillon

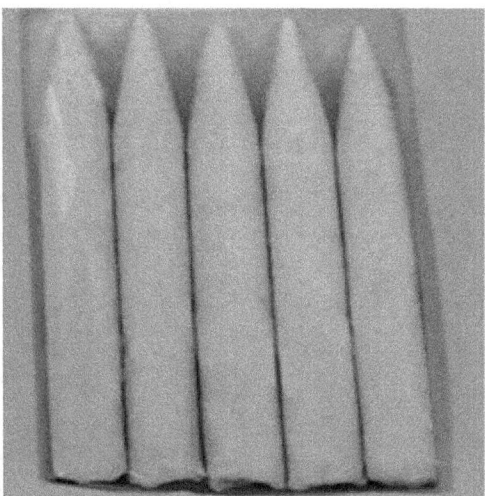

Used to blend your drawing, smear one tone to another (this is the only time you are allowed to smear your work) when making even tones, especially in facial areas. You can use fine sand paper to make polish the pointer, when it's ruin. Also when you use this, position the tortillon at an angle of 45° (Slanting "/") from your working paper.

Bristol Pad or Illustration Board

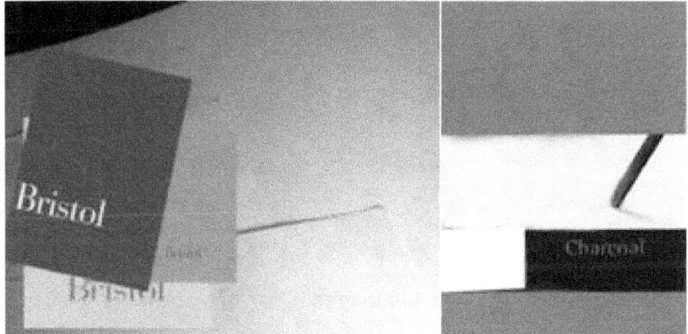

For our drawings Bristol paper will be used, they come in board and pads 2-ply, the front has a Plate surface, a smooth finish and has an egg shell texture, while the back has the Vellum surface texture, I used the Vellum surface which is good for shading. Using Compress Charcoal and adhere more to the surface, comes in different sizes, a good suggestion is to make sure it's marked as acid free(so that your work can last a long time aside from spraying Fixative)..

You can use other type of paper, but make it's the right one for drawing using pencils and Charcoals.

Illustration board is also good for Pencil and Charcoal works, use the cold press since it has tooth and texture, which make the pencil and charcoal adhere to the surface.

Ruler and Template

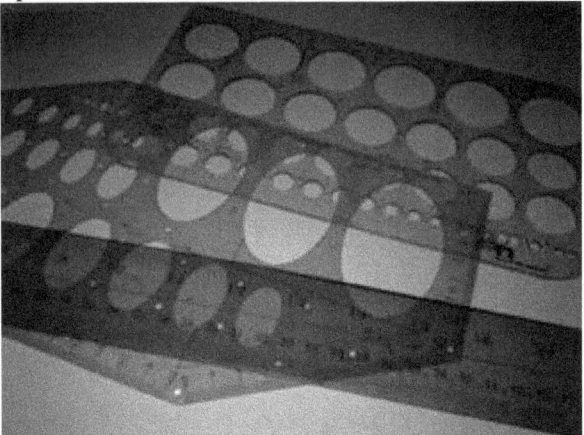

Ruler helps you draw straight lines, measure distance, you can use plastic or wooden for our drawings.

Templates can be use to draw circles or ellipse accurately, especially when drawing the parts of the eyes. Which demand a good form of shape.

Plastic Container

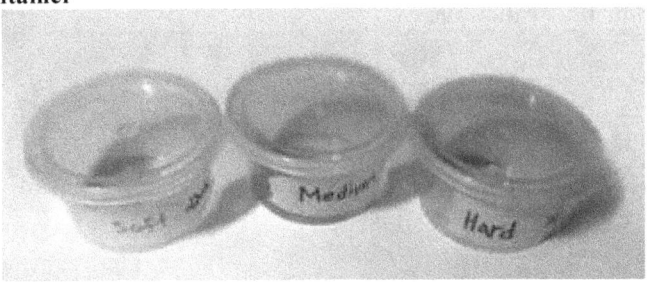

Serve as your container for your accumulated dust, after shaving the charcoal.

Magnifying Lens

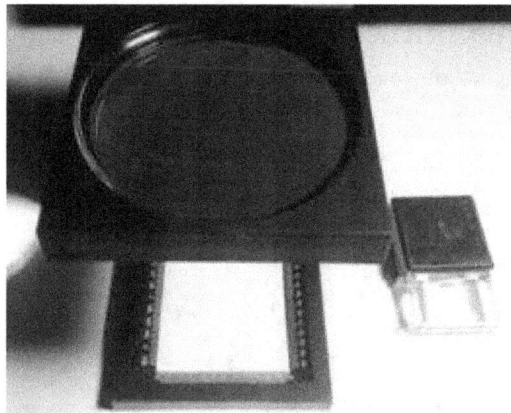

To magnify the image you are copying, so that your work will have more details; since we want it to look real.

Dusting Brush

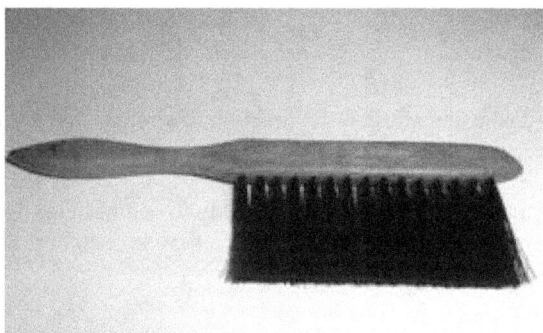

Use to take unwanted dirt and eraser particles in your work, and keep your work clean.

Shaving the Charcoal

So, before I teach you how to render using Charcoal. Let me show you how to shave the Charcoal using cutter first.

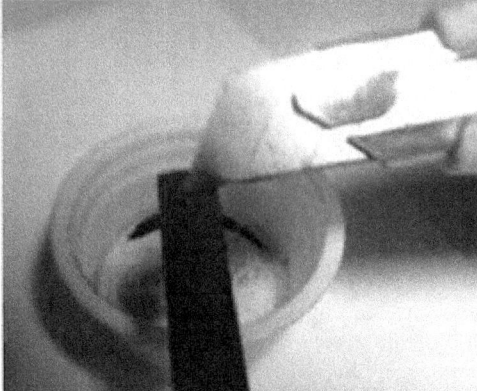

Shave your Charcoal using a one -way direction of strokes where you place it to your container or cup to accumulate the dust or powder to use.

So now we have a Charcoal dust and we're ready to begin, Lets copy the outline of the sphere from our previous exercise or make a new sphere for this exercise.

Rendering Using Charcoal

For Charcoal they are similar to pencils, but there is difference in terms shading, since you're going to use brush to fill the values (more area coverage), unlike using pencil which you have to make a lot of strokes to fill a specific area.

And Charcoal has a darker values compare to Pencil even with various ranges of tones; also Charcoal has a matte texture unlike Pencil it Glossy in texture.

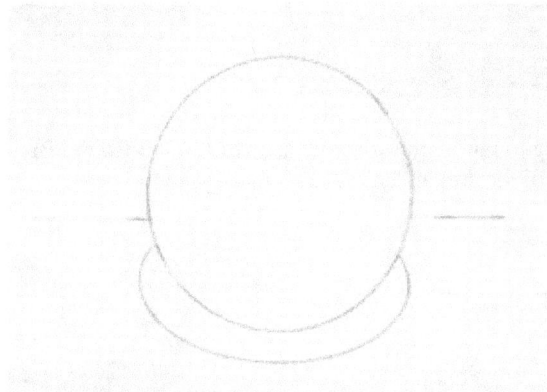

Draw a light circle inside the sphere; this would be our guide when rendering the shadow.

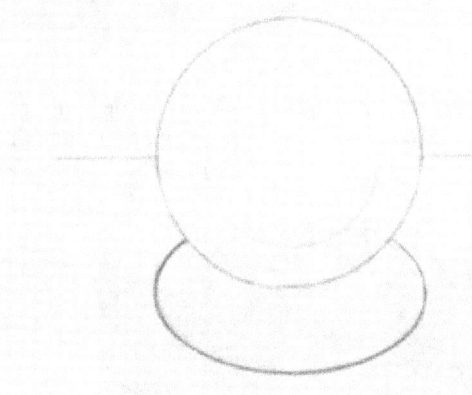

Let's use the Soft Charcoal, which has a darkest tone to the cast shadow, use your Small Flat Brush and fill the area with a pressure enough to make a tone; the stroke should be the same when shading with Pencil or Tortillon.

Note: Tap your brush 2-3 times in the container to remove excess Charcoal dust in your brush before applying it in your working paper.

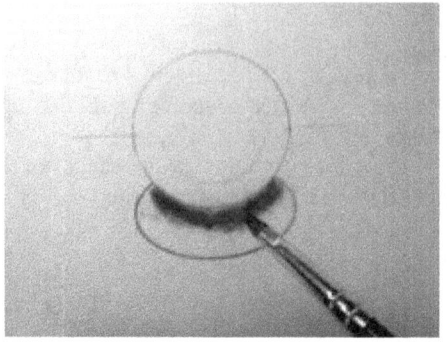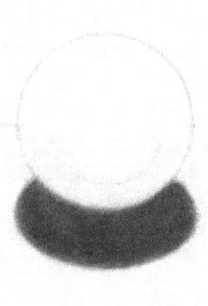

Next we're going to render the shadow, use your Small Round Brush and with dabbing stroke fill the area in a circular motion going up.

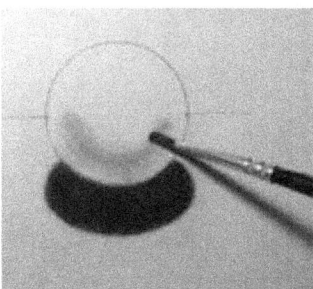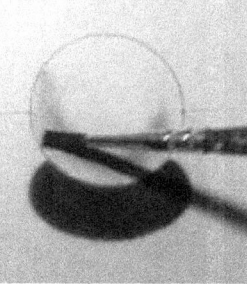

Then it's time to focus on the reflected light, get your kneaded eraser and mold it to point shape, and lightly erase some tone in a circular motion, enough to have a reflected light tone.

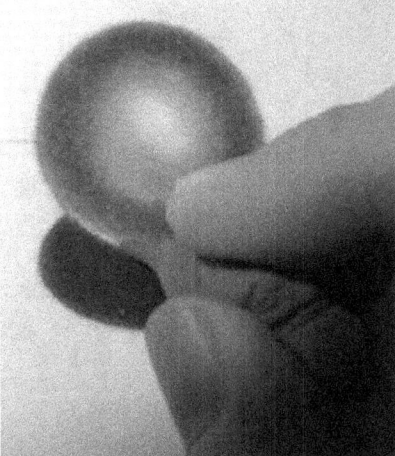

Erase the Charcoal dust outside the Sphere also clean your work using dusting brush.

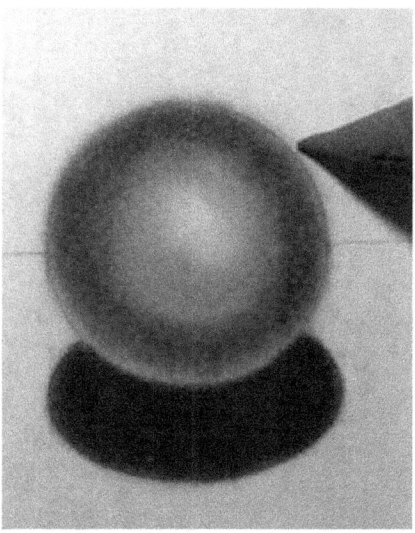

Time to render the ground, where our sphere is placed. Use your Small Round Brush and dabb some Medium Charcoal beside the sphere and fill the area.

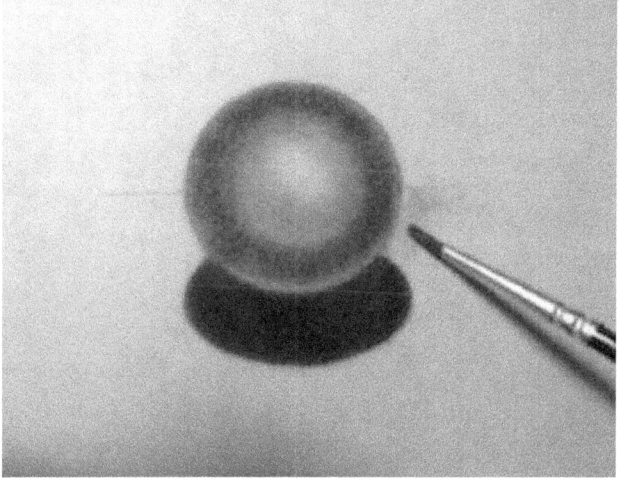

Add the highlights, by lifting some tones using your kneaded eraser.

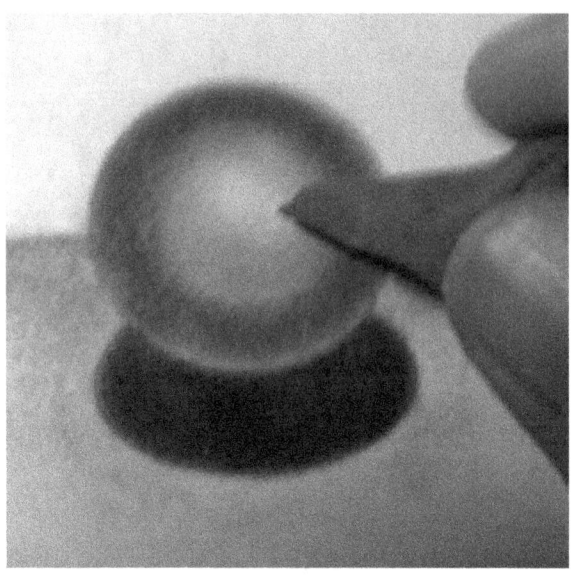

Finish Perfect, we just render a Sphere using Charcoal.-"FANTASTIC"

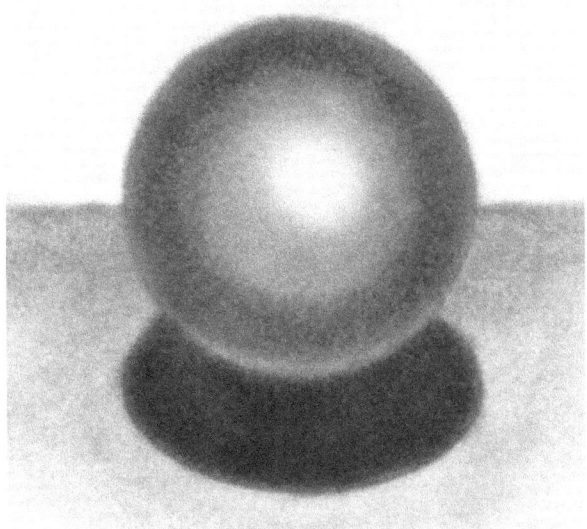

As you can see in the illustration, this is how you will likely render portraits, shadows depends on the source of lights, also your very own observation of shadow from their respective shapes, will help you in your drawing in achieving realism. Remember that value of tones changes as the object moves away the light.

Application

Drawing an Outline

Outline is line of the shape of the object; other says that it is a mark of a boundary.

Grid System

If you find it difficult to draw the outline accurately, not to worry we have solution to that, "The Grid System", used by a German Artist named Albrecht Durer, he created this device to assist artist when drawing details, also by this he can re-scale his work. We don't need that device, what you will just make a grid measure 1/2" over the picture of the subject, and draw a desired inches of grid on your paper, same squares with picture of the subject, copy the picture from the Grid to your drawing paper, after that erase the grid in your working paper, Also I have to mention it would be better that the picture was a photocopy or scanned. Not to ruin the original picture.

Tracing Table or Light Table / Flexi-glass with Bendable Lamp

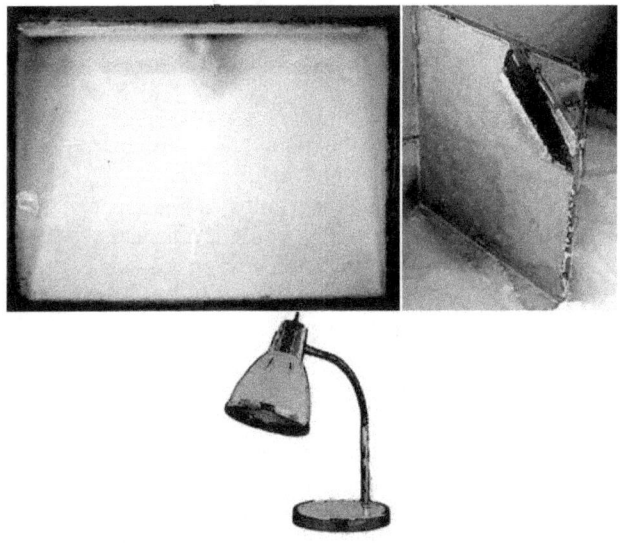

Aside from the grid system, we have an equipment that we can use for drawing outline, and let me mention the disadvantage of the grid system, the problem is that after erasing the grid in your working paper, it leave some mark from erasure that ruin the texture of paper, the solution is to use "Tracing Table or Light Table " with this you don't need to make a grid anymore, you just need a copy or print of your subject in any scale: place it on the tracing table, with your working paper over it ("on the top of it") and trace the image. If ever you don't have a Tracing Table, you can improvise by using a clear Flexi-glass, ¼" thick and size that can accommodate your work, On a Horizontal Position (you can use chairs or anything that will support the Flexi-glass in that position), Place a bendable Lamp under it, turn it on (the idea is to place the light source at the back of the Flexi-glass so you can use it like a tracing table), mount the picture or print of the subject and your working paper over the Flexi-glass, and you have a tracing equipment, very simple that can save you Space, Time and Money. I see others made this kind of tracing table using ordinary box instead of finding chairs for support, so be creative.

Tips to Remember

- o You must have a clear copy or photograph of your subject.
- o See through shapes including the negative of the image as well the positive, to help you visualize the shapes.

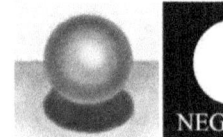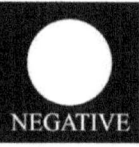

NEGATIVE   POSITIVE

o   Practice sketching simple basic shapes, it will help you improve your strokes and good hand coordination, and it can give you confidence in your work.
o   Sometimes some parts in the photograph are blurred and it's hard to distinguish, in that case, use your imagination.
o   It's not bad, to pick up some magazines and newspaper, and find a picture you want to draw and also interest you, for practice.
o   Secure yourself a good lighting source when drawing.
o   Watch the proportion of shapes to other shapes in a picture.
o   Remember different textures have different technique or strokes, that you need imitate when drawing.
o   If you find some parts of the face and other parts of the body, difficult to draw, break it down to smaller components.
o   It helps if you have reference in handy or take photograph, so that you will have a guide when drawing and shading, especially if your confuse of the shadows and cast shadow in your drawing.
o   If you're having issues with smudges or fingerprints cause by oil from your hand on your work, you can prevent this by placing an extra sheet of paper under your working hand specifically the side of your palm.
o   Constant practice drawing and rendering, for sure will make you succeed.

Exercises

Zebra

As this is our first exercise, take a look of the picture of the zebra below; take note of the shapes, tones of the body, the light source as well the transition of tones, and the contents in the background, middle-ground and foreground (subject). I assure you this is easy, so let's start.

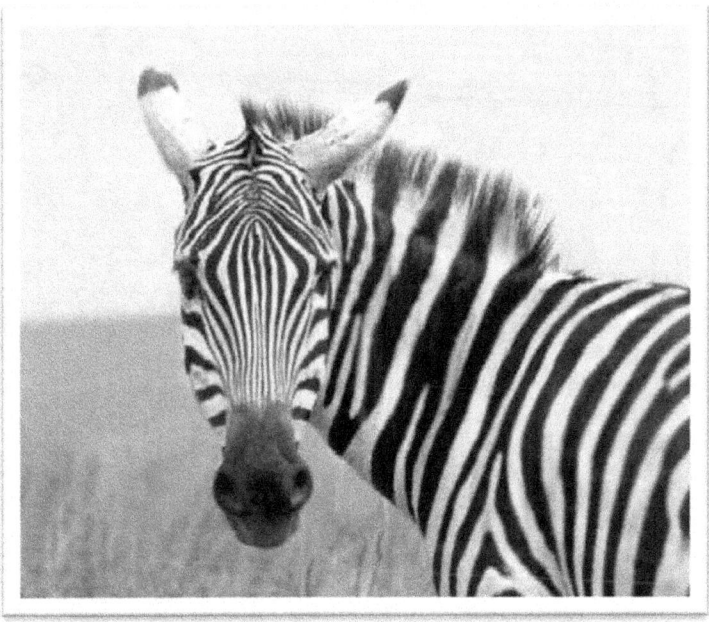

Copy the outline below to your Bristol Pad or Illustration board, or you may scan it using your scanner and enlarge it, after mount it to the Tracing Table or Light Table / Flexi-glass with Bendable Lamp and place your Working paper (Bristol Pad or Illustration board) over it and trace the outline. That's it very simple.

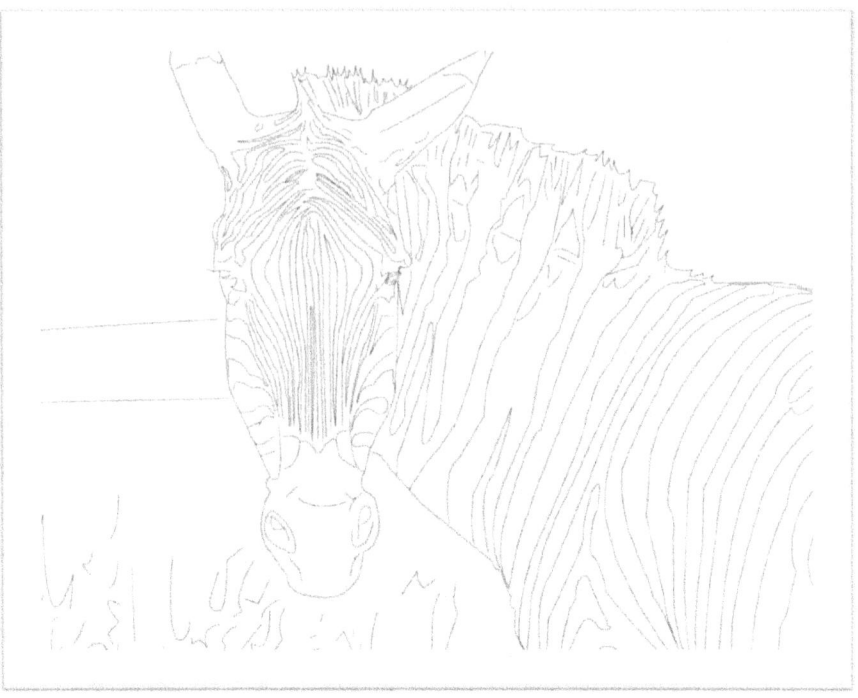

Steps:

1. Using Soft Charcoal S. with Flat Brush, apply it to the stripes on the body of the Zebra; use the method we used in rendering Sphere. And also apply it to dark areas: hairs, dark tone above the ears, eyes, and nostrils.

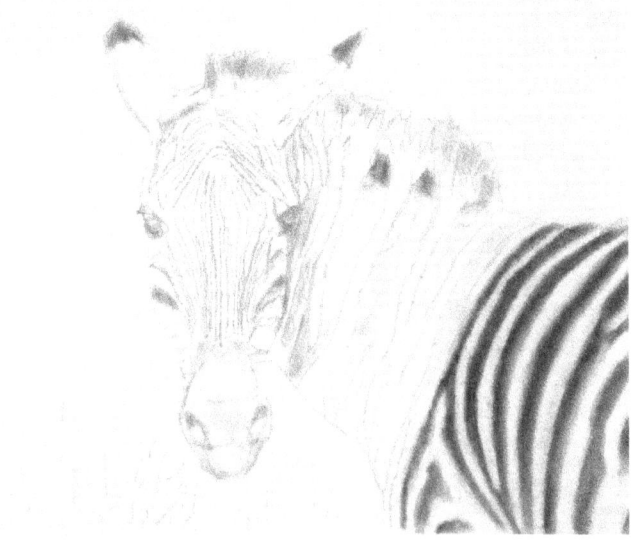

2.   Continue applying the tone to the rest of the Stripes, take note of how the value varies there are dark and light tones, dark tone requires a heavy pressure and light tones use light pressure, a heavy pressure- the brush is almost close to the paper while for the light- only tip of the brush is touching the paper.

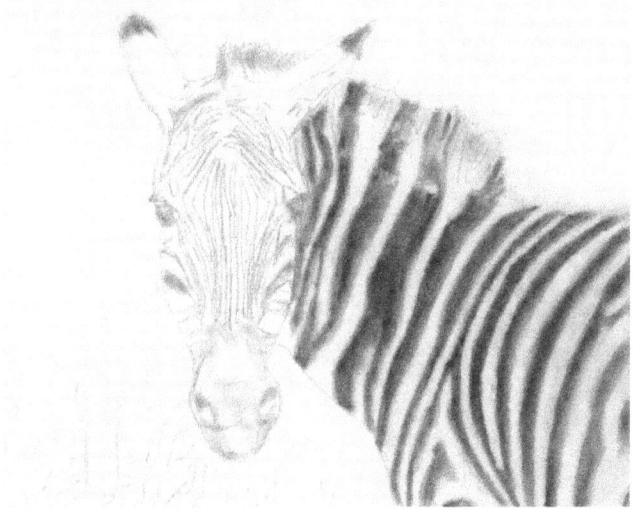

3.   Next apply Medium Charcoal S. with Flat brush, in the stripes on the face

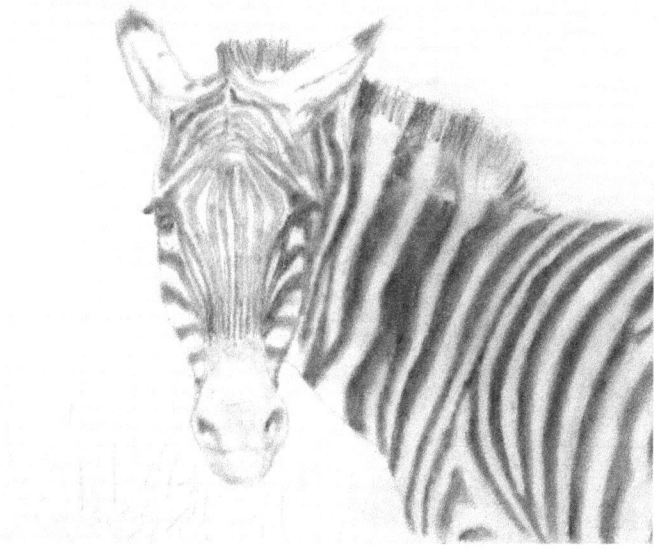

4. Finish the snout by shading it the same charcoal we used in Step 3. take note of the transition or how the light appears in the snout shape, so render it with light pressure.

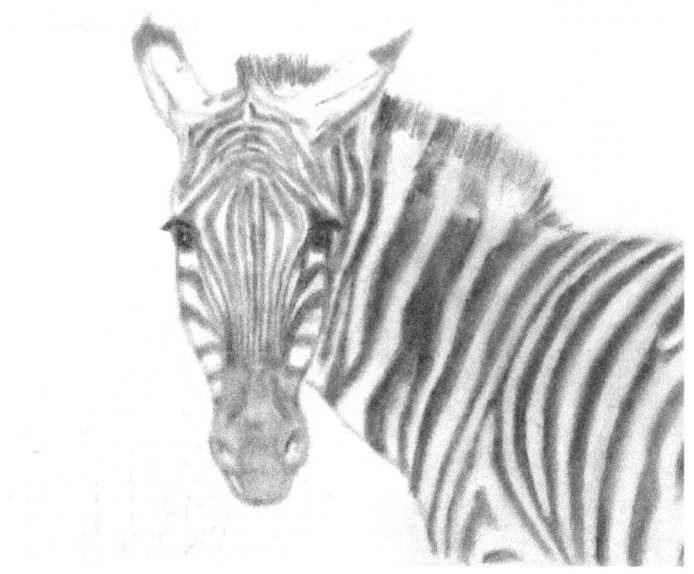

5. Finish the rest of the details using the Medium Charcoal Pencil: hair, ear, face, nose, and snout. Also apply highlights using kneaded eraser (just pull up some charcoal to make the white of the paper appear) eyes, nose, snout and ears.

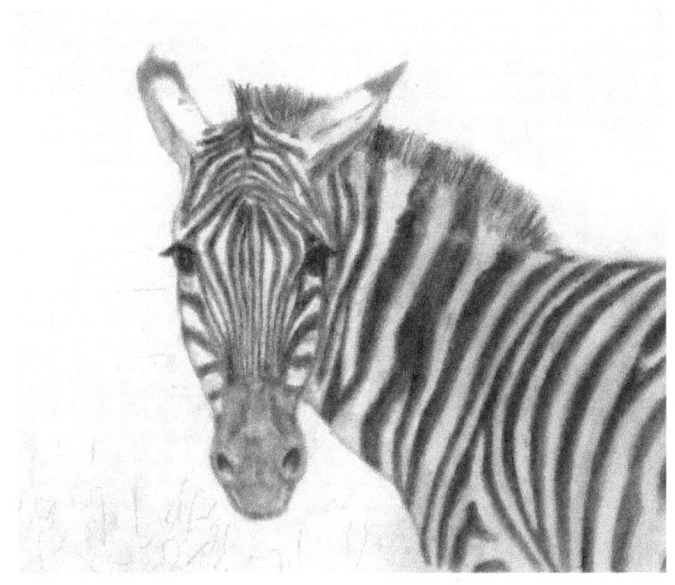

6.   Let's work the details:
- For the sky dab a Hard Charcoal S. using the Round Brush,
- For the Mountain –dab using a Medium Charcoal S. again with Round Brush.
- For the field (middle-ground)- use Medium Charcoal S. with Flat Brush apply it by shading it horizontally,

Apply highlights on the line between the mountain and field

- For the bushes near the foreground- use Medium and Soft Charcoal S. to render it using vertical strokes. Add highlights using kneaded eraser to add an effects.

After that check for any corrections, add a tone if needed,and if you see that you applied a very dark tone to the light area erase it using your eraser. When finished spray fixative to your work and we're finished take a break before starting the next exercise.

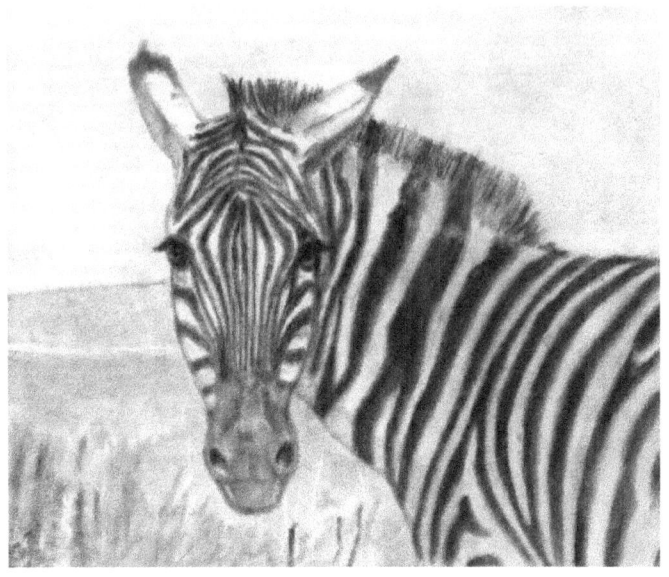

This is how it's really looks like if finished and with light over it.

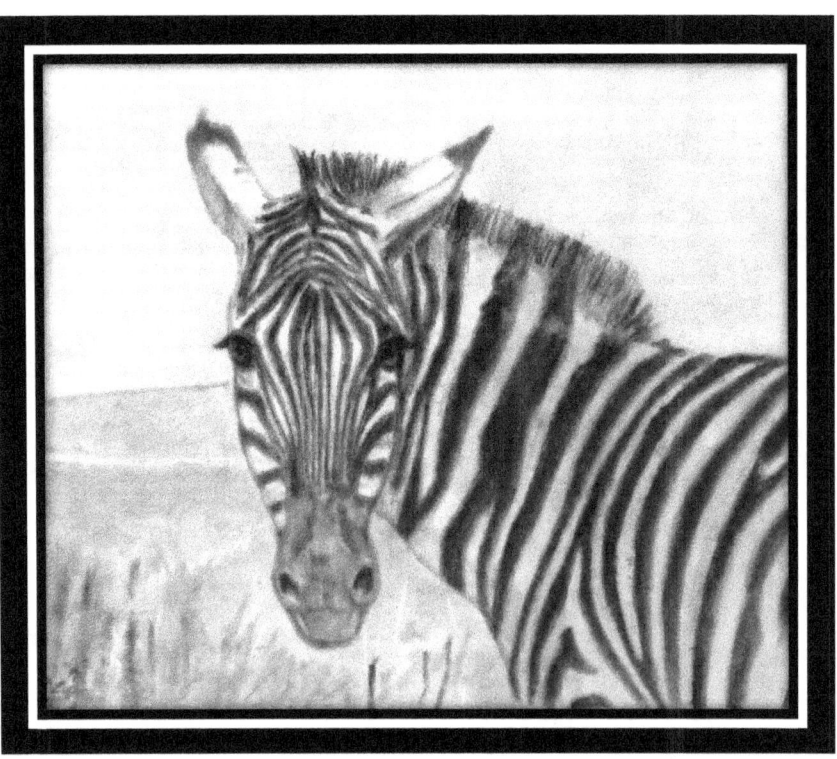

Giraffe

We're now in our second animal, our long neck friend looks so challenging to render, like the Zebra in our fist exercise, and they have distinctive patterns in their body, now before we start, imagine first how you will render this Giraffe, watch the shapes and take notes of the transition of the values.

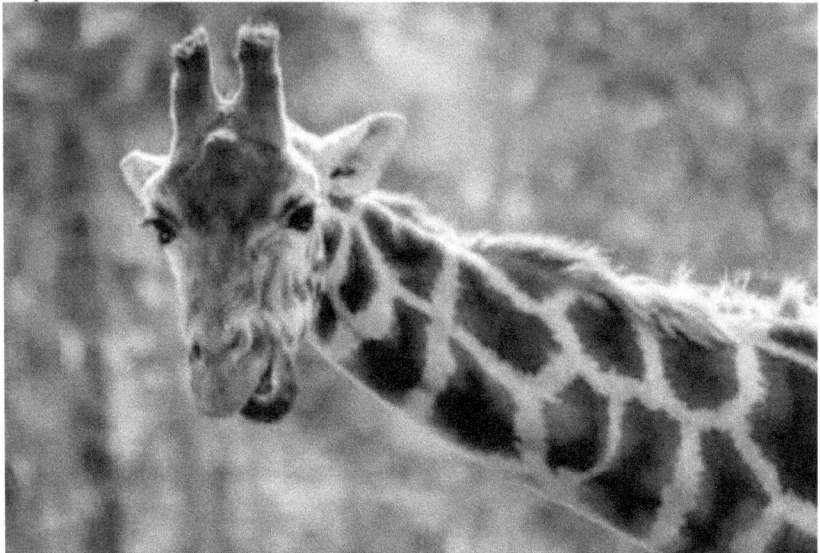

Transfer the outline to your working paper, the same method we used when we transferred the image of the Zebra.

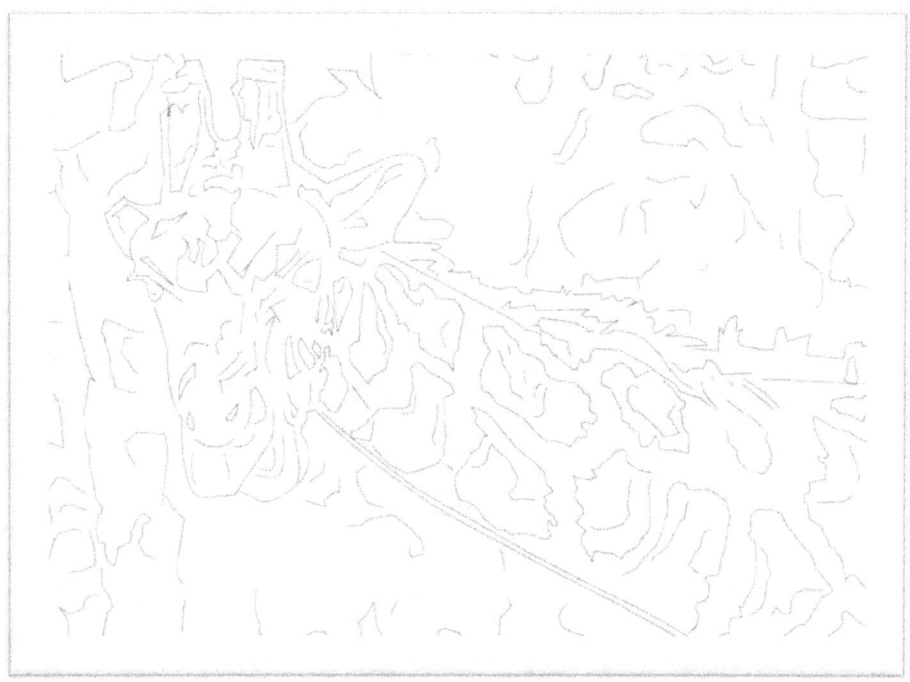

Steps:
1. Identify the Dark areas first, and using your Soft Charcoal S. with Flat Brush, shade it to those areas: inside the patterns or markings.

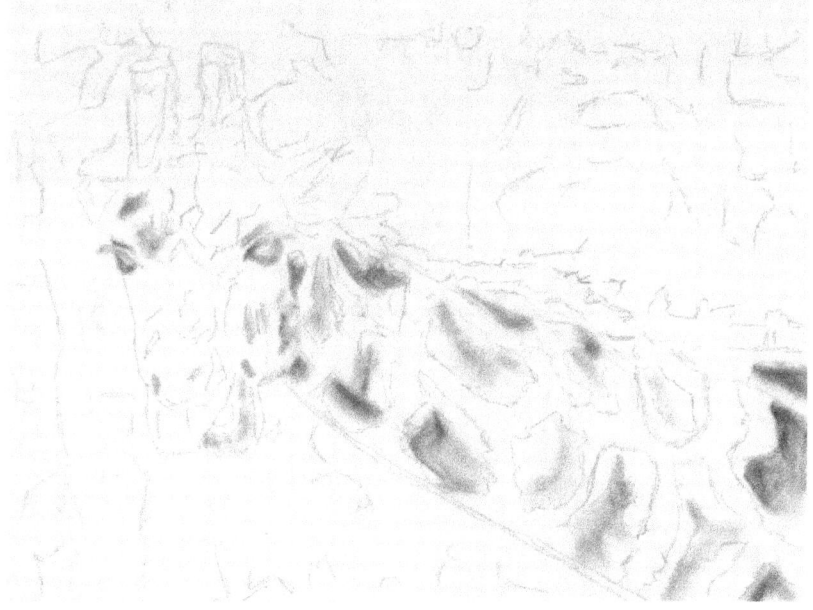

2. Next is to shade the side of those pattern with Medium Charcoal S. again with Flat Brush, and also tone the face and the horns with this Medium Charcoal tone with light pressure (if you are not confident with the pressure you're using practice if first to another paper, if you have enough practice then that's the time to apply it to your actual work-light and heavy pressure; light has light tone while the heavy tone has darker tone).

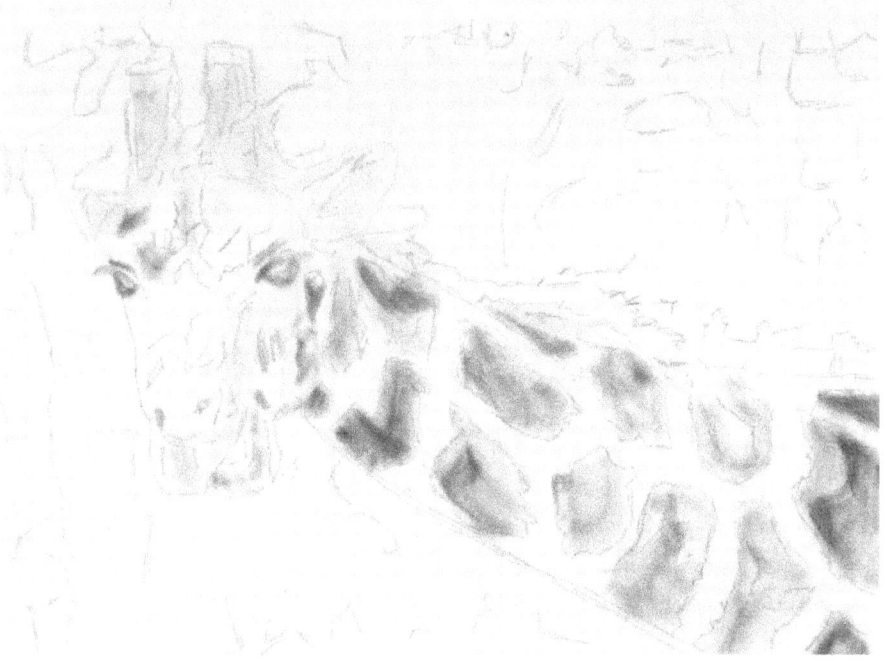

3. Tone the neck with Hard Charcoal S. using Round Brush.

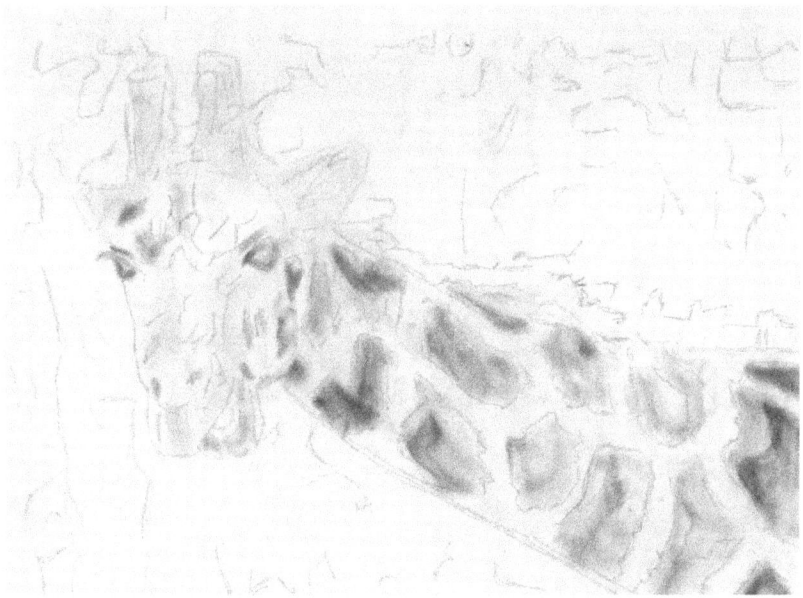

4. Add more definition to the face, by shading the face with Charcoal S. and using Charcoal Pencils, start using Dark Charcoal going to Light Charcoal. So the orientation should be Charcoal: Soft>Medium>Hard S. /Pencil (for tight and thin areas). Below is the guide of what to Shade to the areas.
   A. Soft Charcoal Shave
   B. Medium Charcoal Shave
   C. Hard Charcoal Shave

   Match the areas with tones you see below, you may apply another layer if needed.

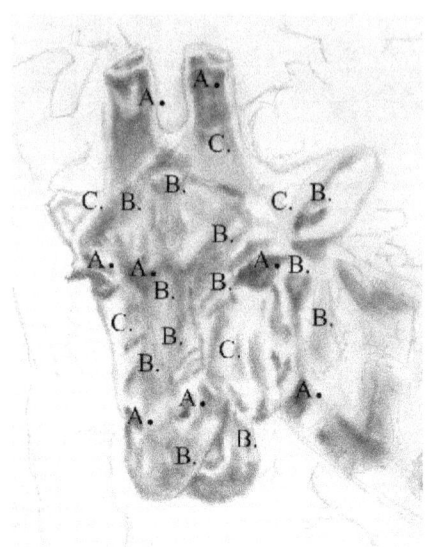

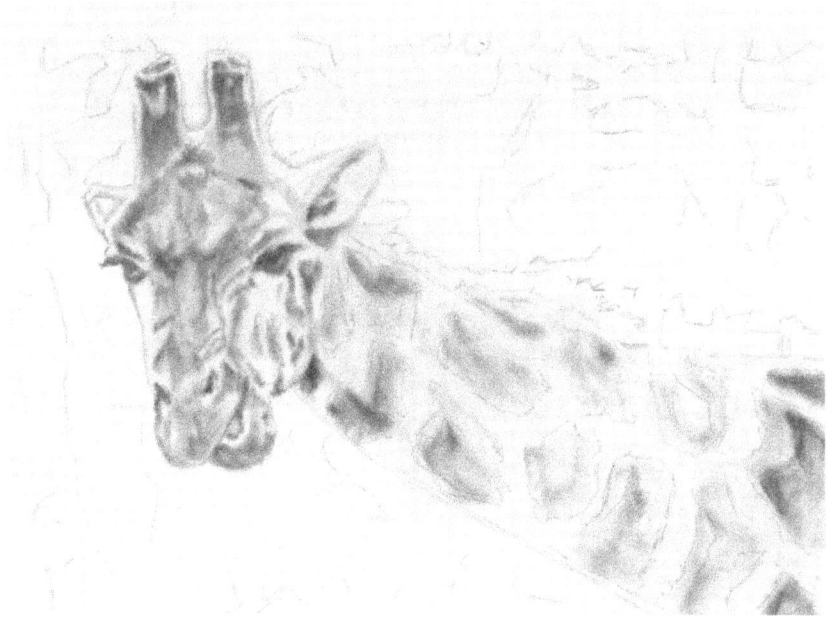

5. Now time to work the neck, add more tone to the patches, apply another coat of Medium Charcoal S. to the light areas of the patches to make it more darker than before, also render the hair on the top of the neck, again use Soft Charcoal S. to dark areas, and shade the outline with Medium Charcoal S. or another trick is to draw the outline using Medium Charcoal Pencil and blend it with your Tortillon to make it soft edge. Apply highlights on the eyes, ears, nose, and lower lip below the neck.

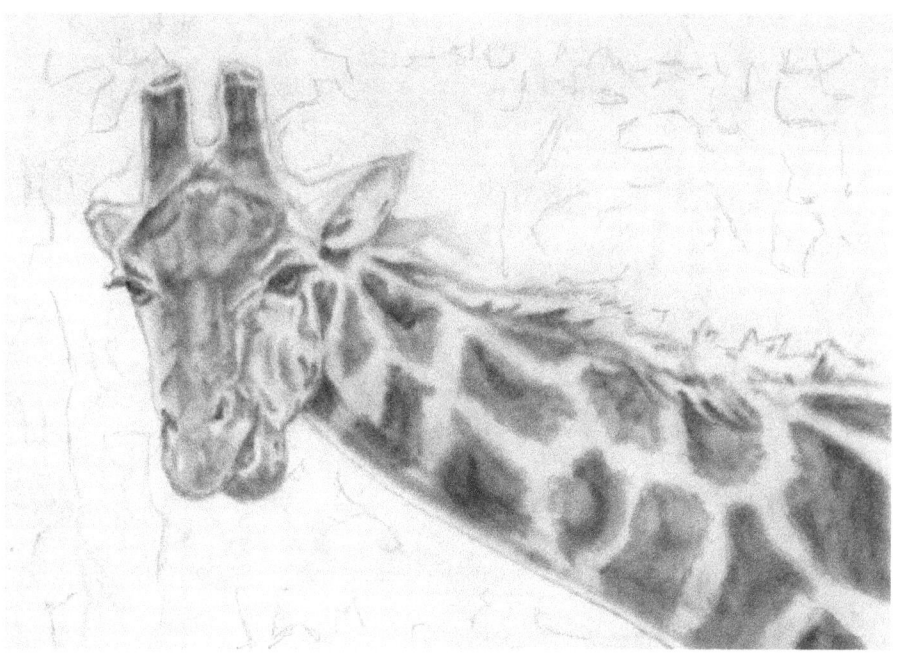

6.   Finish the background: Start shading the entire background with Lightest
      Value by dabbing it with Hard Charcoal S. with Large Round Brush, next
      apply dark values to the dark areas with Soft Charcoal S. using your Flat
      Brush use the picture below as a guide, and lastly dab a Medium Value
      using a Medium Charcoal S. to some areas to make it more diffuse or soft
      edge.
      Check for any corrections and after that spray it with fixative.

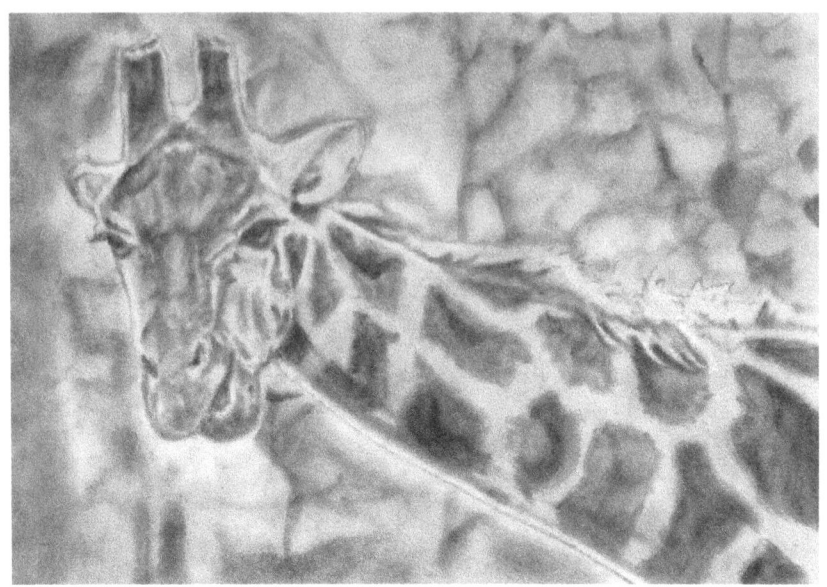

As you can see, the picture below looks alive.

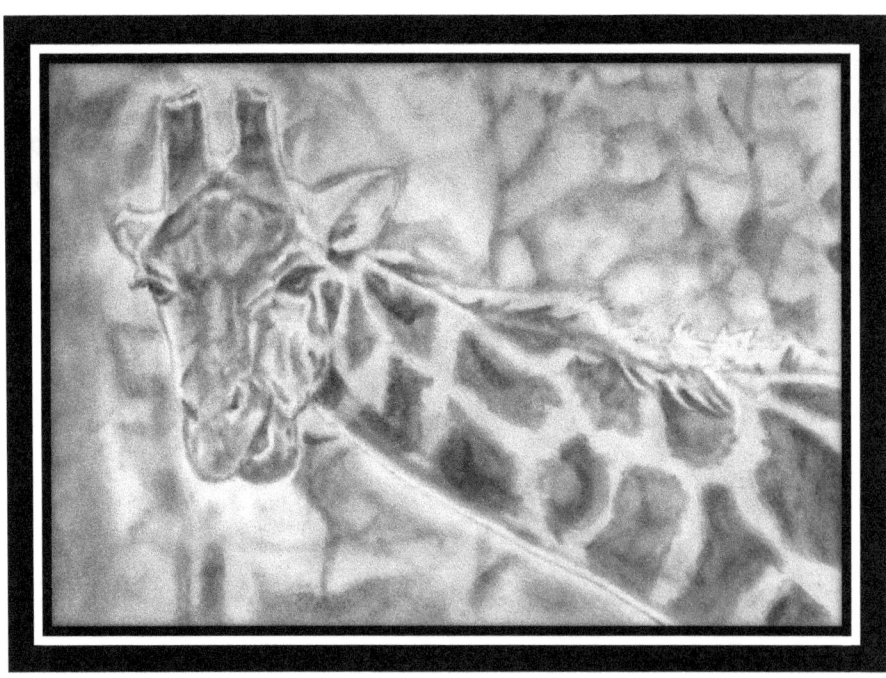

Elephant

For our third exercise, let's render this heavy mammal, who likes peanut, also for this challenge we're going to render it focus on its body texture as well the background. And don't forget to study the picture below before you begin.

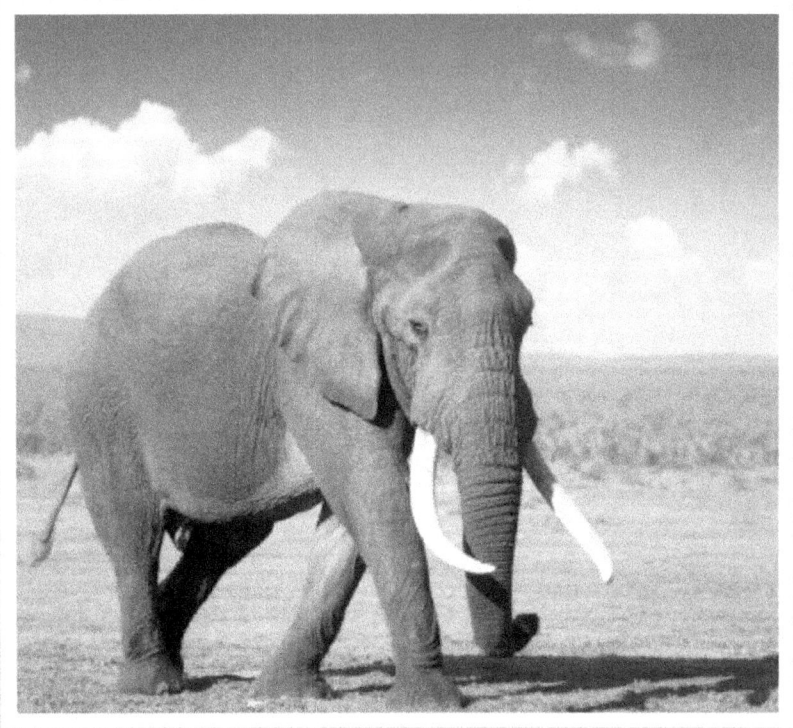

Again transfer this outline to your working paper, and we're set to go.

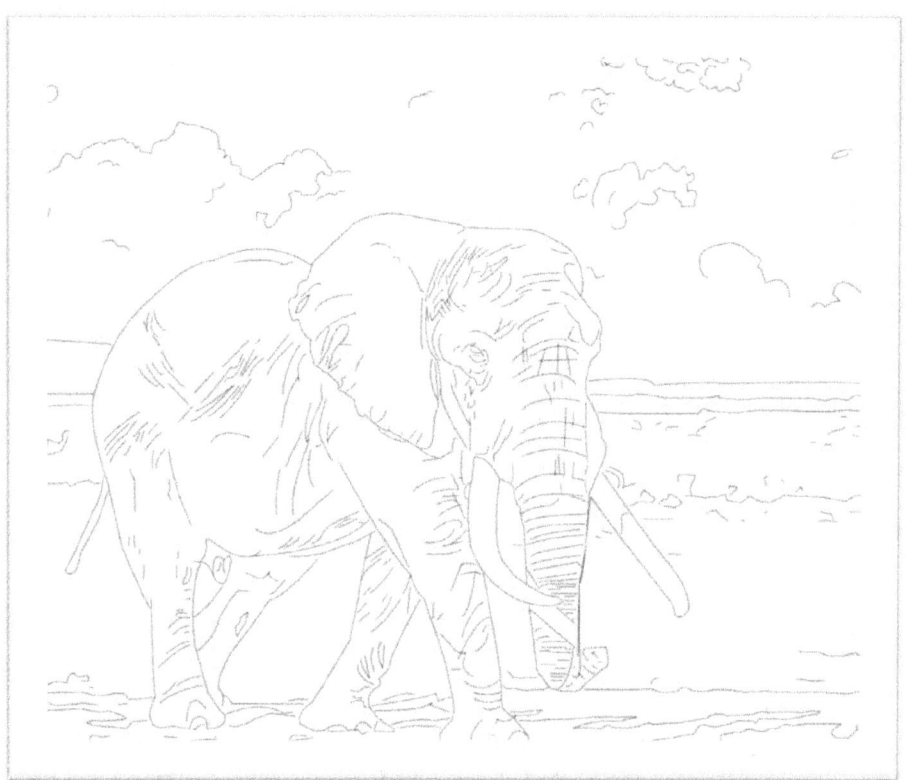

Steps:
1. Begin Shading the Dark areas, using the Soft Charcoal S. with your Flat Brush: left hind leg, shadow on the right ear and shadow on the left face. And shade the shadow with the same Charcoal tone but use light pressure for this to be safe you can another layer later.

2. To see the right contrast at this early stage we can begin working the background, using the guide below use Charcoal shave with Large Round Brush, use dabbing strokes when rendering the sky, work slowly but surely and working with the consistency of the value as well a good transition from dark(soft Charcoal) to light(hard Charcoal).

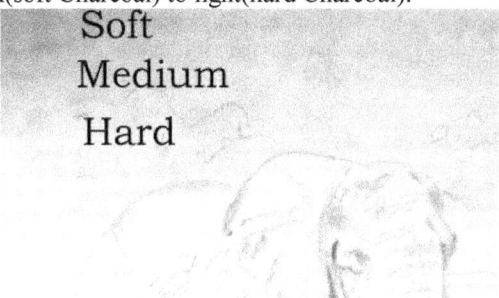

Soft

Medium

Hard

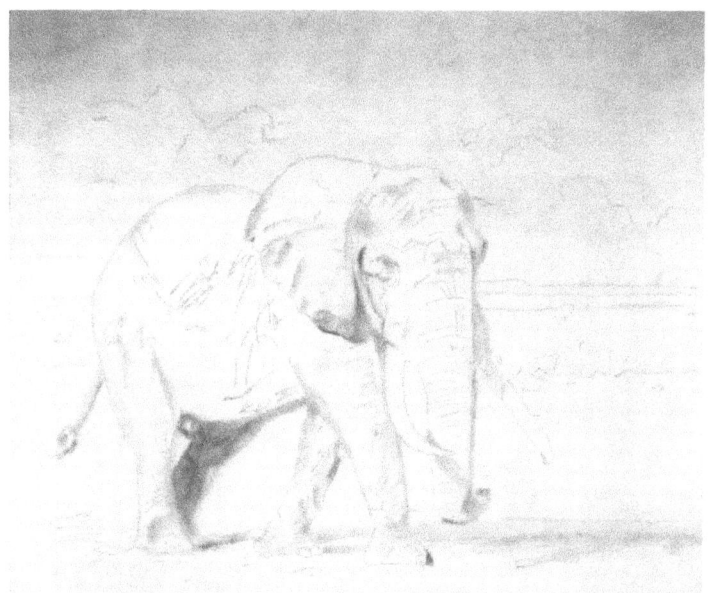

3. Next is to render the clouds in the sky, you can use your Vinyl eraser but if you have an electric eraser the better- it can erase deeper making the white of the paper more visible compared to any other eraser.

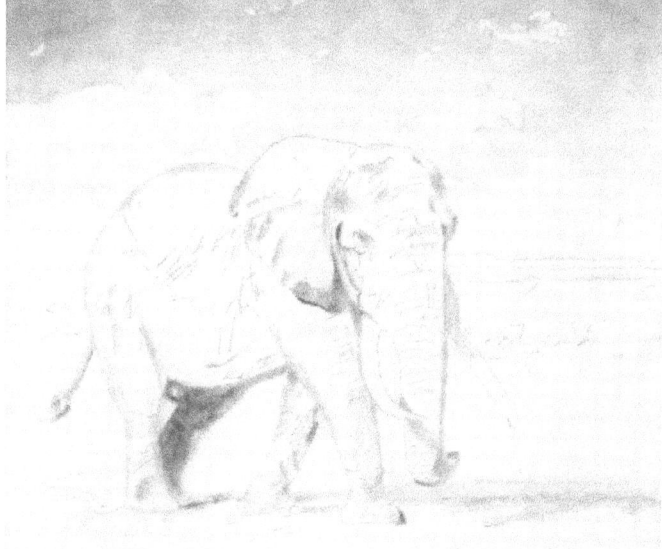

4. Finish the rest of the background using the guide below:
    A. Soft Charcoal S. with Flat Brush, use light pressure.
    B. Hard Charcoal S. with Round Brush
    C. Medium Charcoal S. with Round Brush

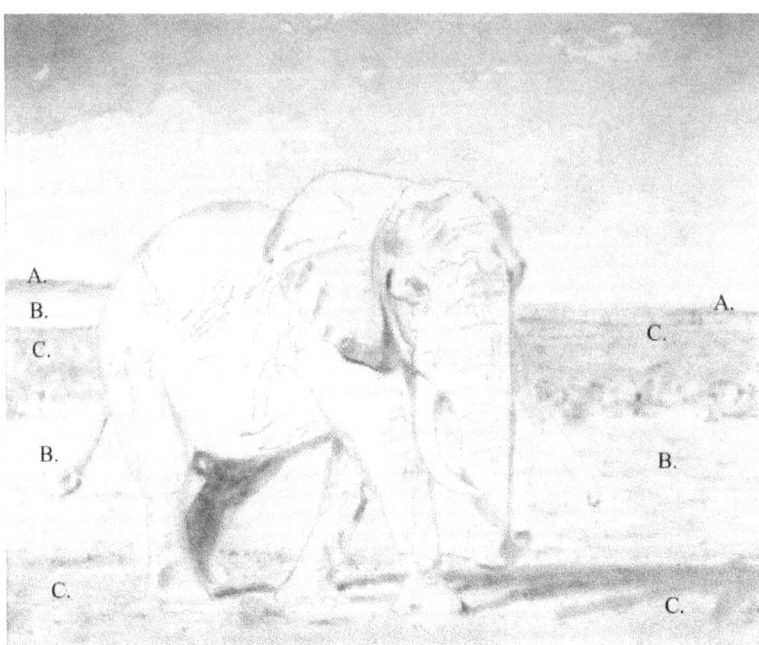

Note: For the middle ground area with C. add details using Medium Charcoal Pencil to add some effects and blend it with Tortillon to soften, for B. areas details draw light thin and short horizontal random lines with Medium Charcoal Pencil and again soften it with Tortillon.

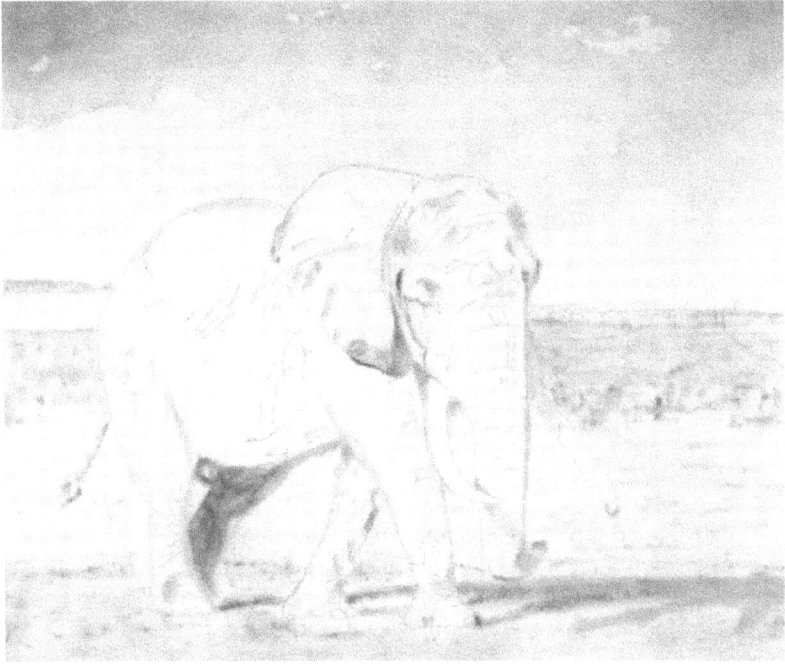

5.   Finish the details and texture of the subject:

First   Apply tone the body of the elephant by dabbing a Hard Charcoal S. with Round Brush.

Second Draw details like the eyes, lips and tusks using Hard Charcoal S. and soften it with tortillon, so that it will not look so sharp.

Third   Next add wrinkles to the following areas using Hard Charcoal Pencil: trunk, ear, body and legs,

Fourth Apply Highlights to the following areas using Kneaded eraser: ears, front face beside the trunk, body, tail and legs.

After you're finished, check your work for any corrections, and then spray it with fixative. And we're done. Wow you had finished half of the exercises in the eBook, good job and give yourself a pat in the back. Now take a break and after that get back and start the fourth exercise.

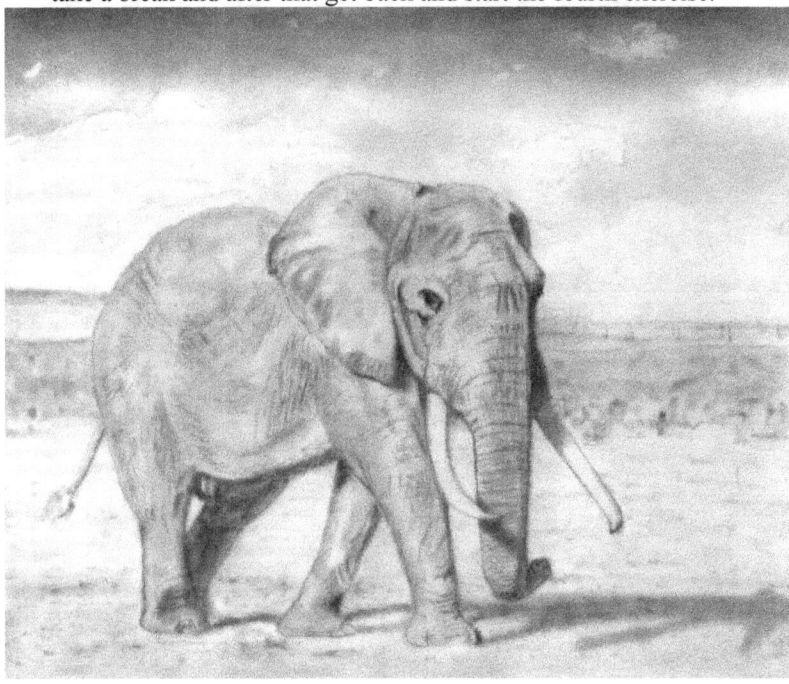

Hey! Look… it's like a scene from a movie, the part where the popular Jungle man calls his elephant ally.

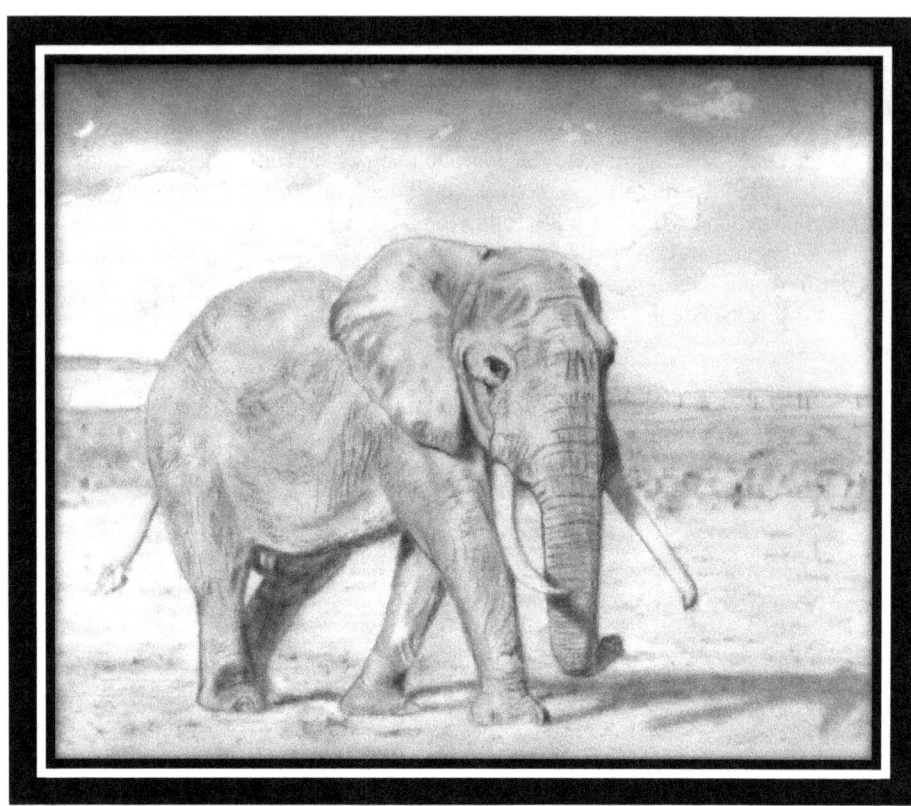

Baby Chimp

For our Fourth exercise let's render this cute little baby Chimp, the challenge is how to render it with consistent even tone, especially with hair covered to its body. Again let me remind you to study the picture first before you begin.

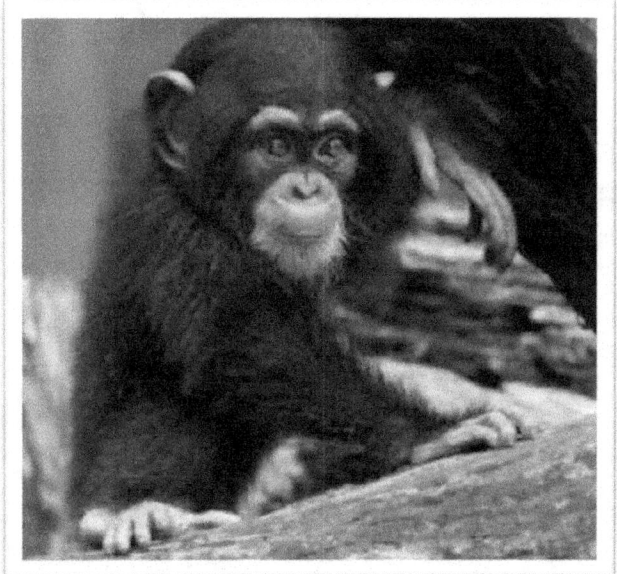

Transfer the outline and I'm sure you know what to do next.

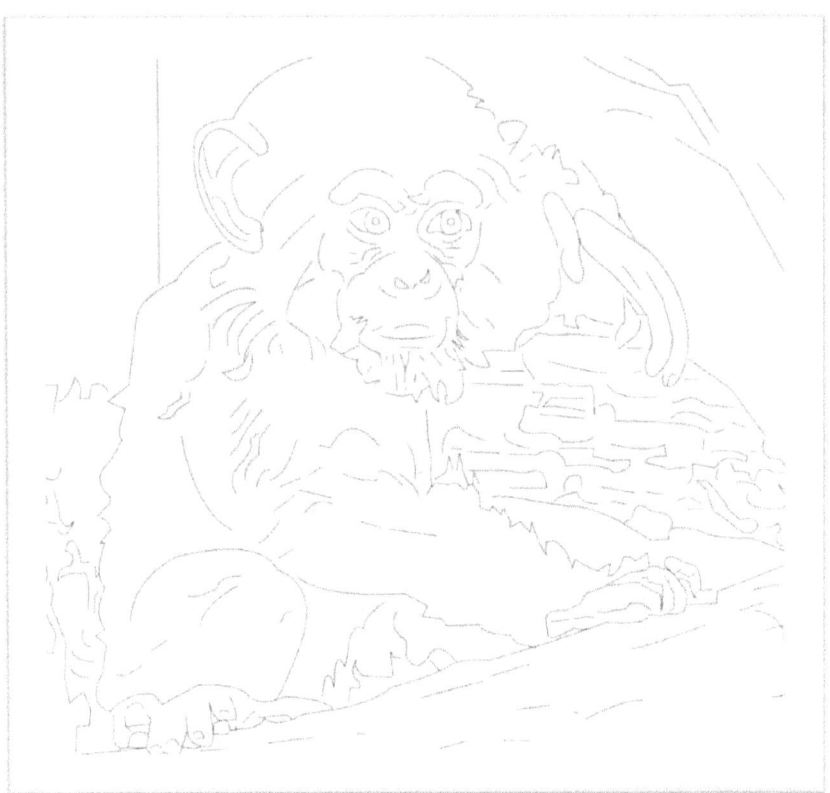

Steps:

1.   Begin in the eyes, apply tone using Soft Charcoal S. (Shaved) with your small Flat Brush around the Iris, copy what you see in the picture below, use your Soft Charcoal Pencil to draw the pupil in the eyes, after that apply the tone to some areas to define the shapes: outline in the head, ears, nose, lips, hand and the body (outer outline) do it lightly so the pressure from your hand would be light also.

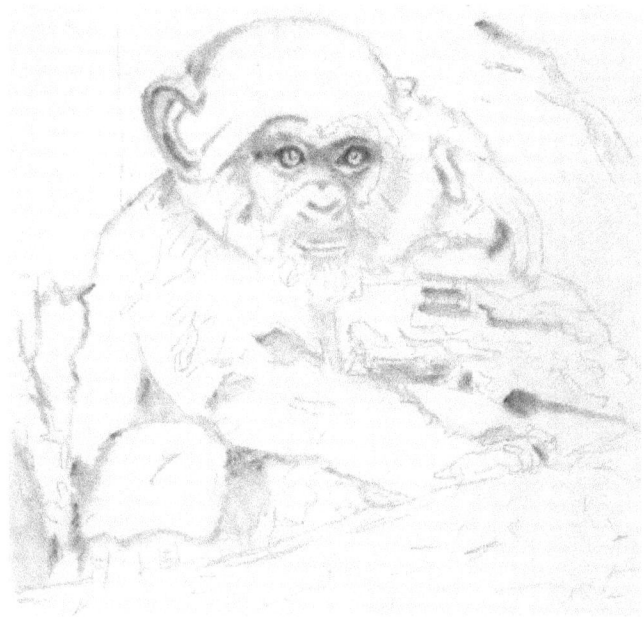

2.   Refine the face by adding more tone using Medium Charcoal S. with your small Round Brush, dab it starting from the side going inward again using light pressure strokes. If you made a mistakes use your kneaded or Vinyl eraser.

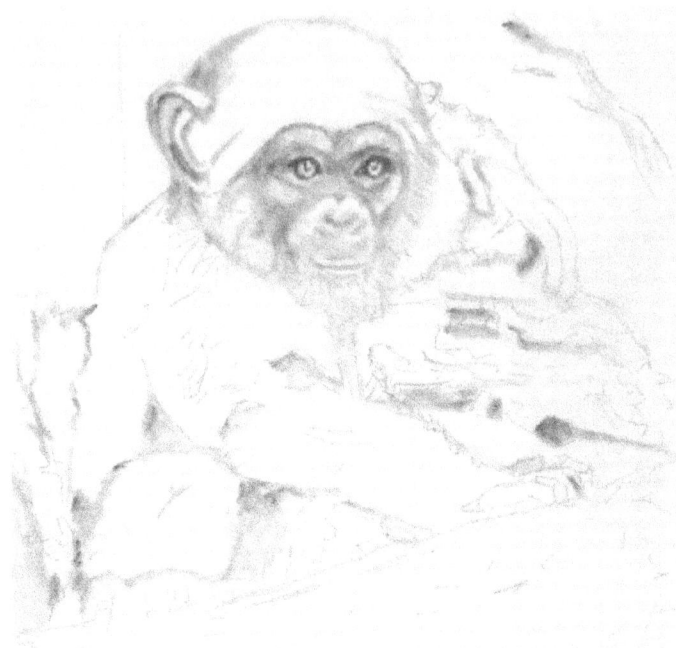

3.   Now apply a Medium Charcoal S. on the top of the head with your Flat
      Brush and sides of the face (hairy side) adding pressure to have a darker
      medium tone.

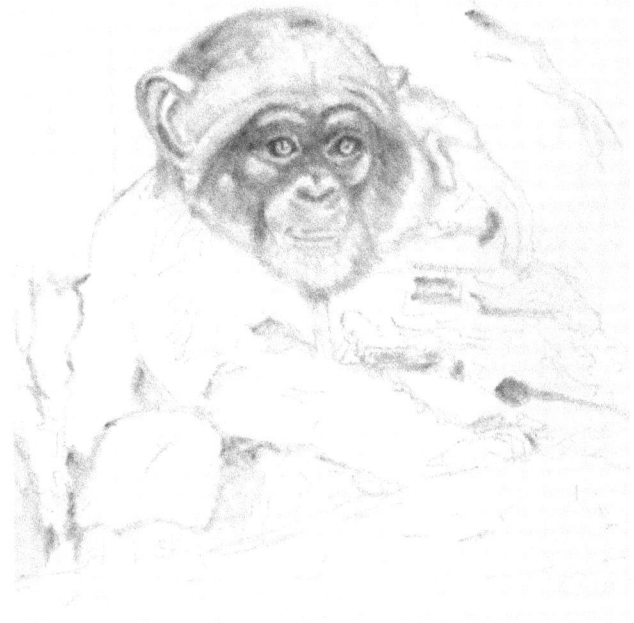

4. Add details using your Medium Charcoal Pencil (make sure that point is sharp to make a thin detail lines). Define shapes by adding tones as what we did before in "Rendering using Charcoal".

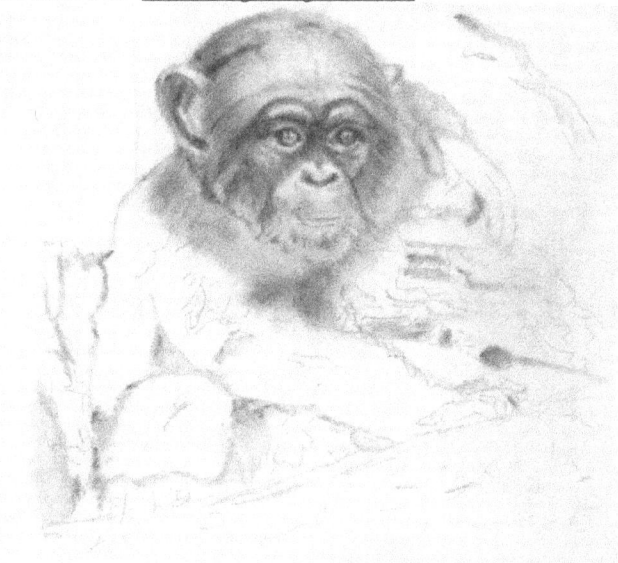

5. Time to render the body, Apply Medium Charcoal S. with Large or Medium Round Brush.

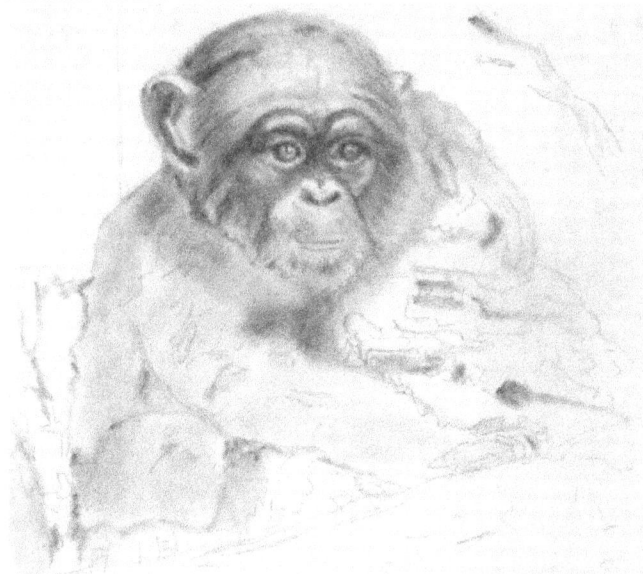

6. To darken the Hair in the body, apply a Soft Charcoal S. with Flat Brush to the dark areas like cast shadows (heavy pressure), and also apply to the rest of the body using same Charcoal but with Round Brush with dabbing strokes(light Pressure).

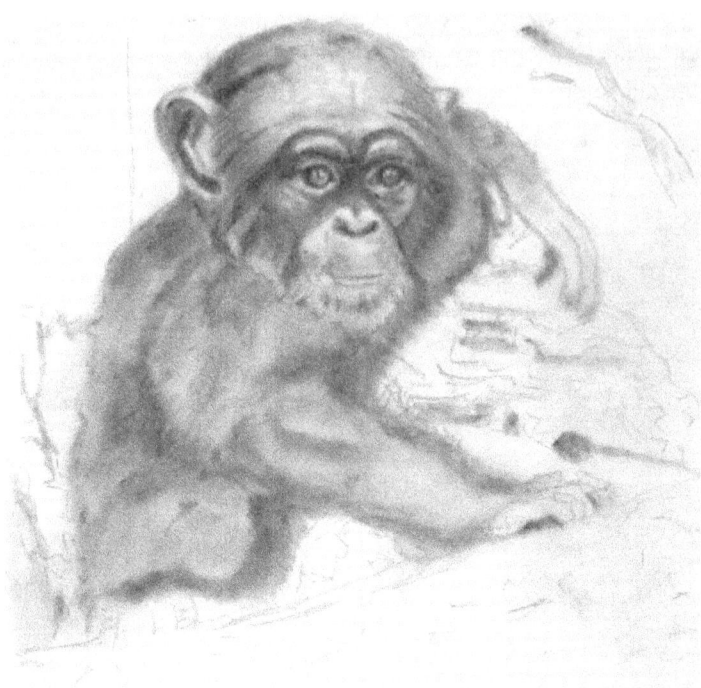

7.   Let's work the background: dab the background with Hard Charcoal S. using large Round Brush for a light tone, then darken the left side with Soft Charcoal S. using Flat Brush and blend it to the light tone using your tortillon, also draw a dark line behind the back of the chimp.

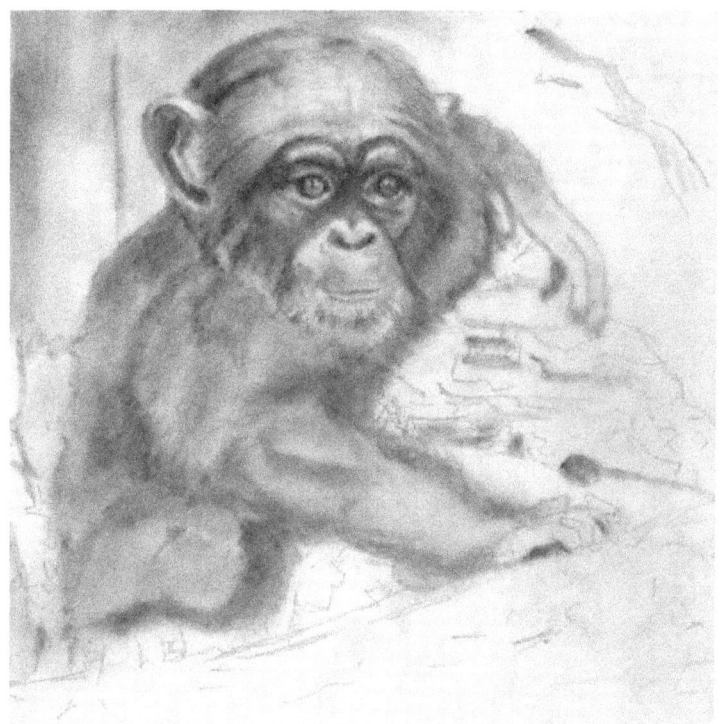

8.   Next would be the middle-ground, dab the area with Hard Charcoal S.,
      again with large Round Brush, using your Medium Charcoal Pencil adds
      the details then shade it with your Flat Brush to make it soft edge (looks
      diffuse), an effect that tells the viewer the depth of the picture. Don't forget
      to fill the dark areas with Soft Charcoal S. or use pencil and just soften it
      with Flat brush with outward strokes.

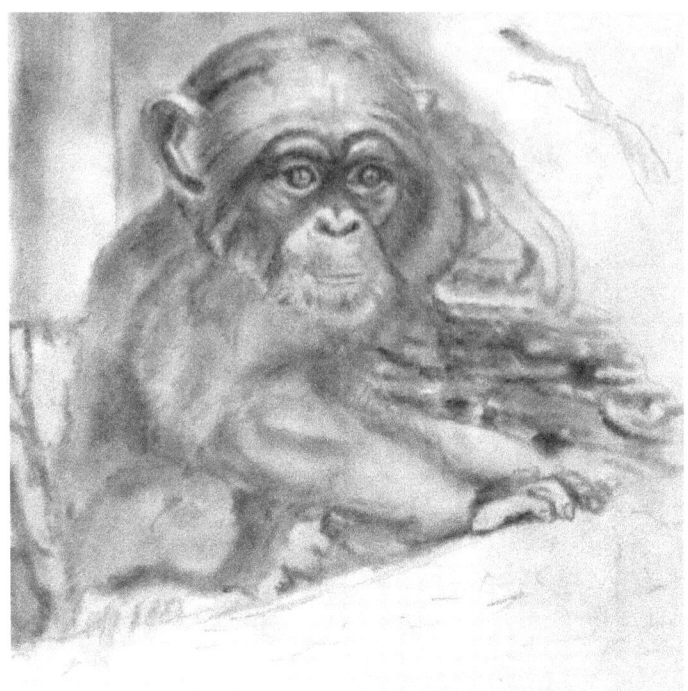

9.   For the foreground(except for the chimp we're going to finish that later),
      Let's darken the dark areas of the branch on the right side by shading it
      using Soft Charcoal S. with Flat Brush and dabbing the rest of the area
      with the same Charcoal but using the round brush. Dab the bottom branch
      with Hard Charcoal S. with Round Brush.

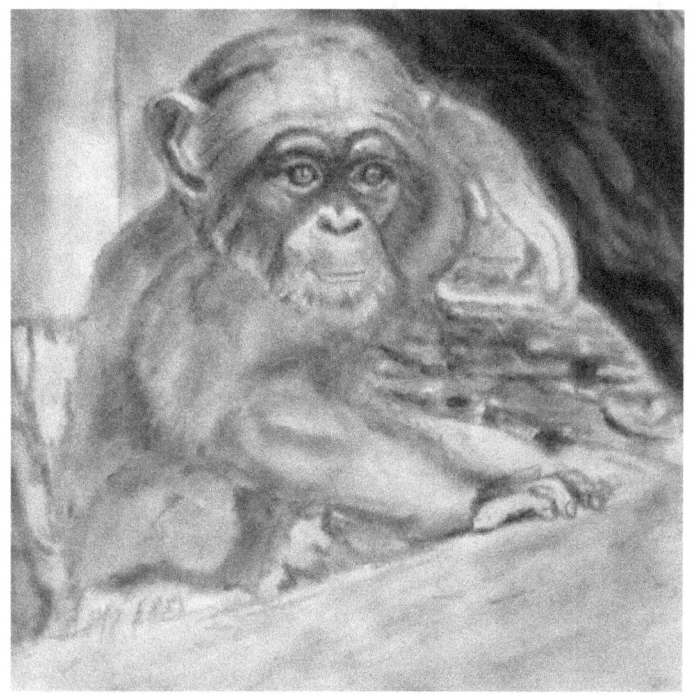

10.   Add details to the branch on the right side, using your kneaded eraser, lift up some tone so that the area will lighten up, note that this is not a highlight but more of a reflected light; you may add a tone lightly to the areas to give texture (a.). Add a highlight to the Top right corner using the Electric eraser (b.).

a. 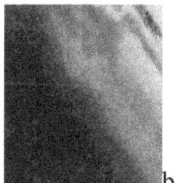b.

For the bottom branch, dab a Medium Charcoal S. with Round Brush to the area near the front, also using your Medium Charcoal Pencil draw some thin diagonal lines to give texture to it, you may thicken some of the lines to have a random texture, after that add highlights diagonally and some dots using kneaded Eraser.

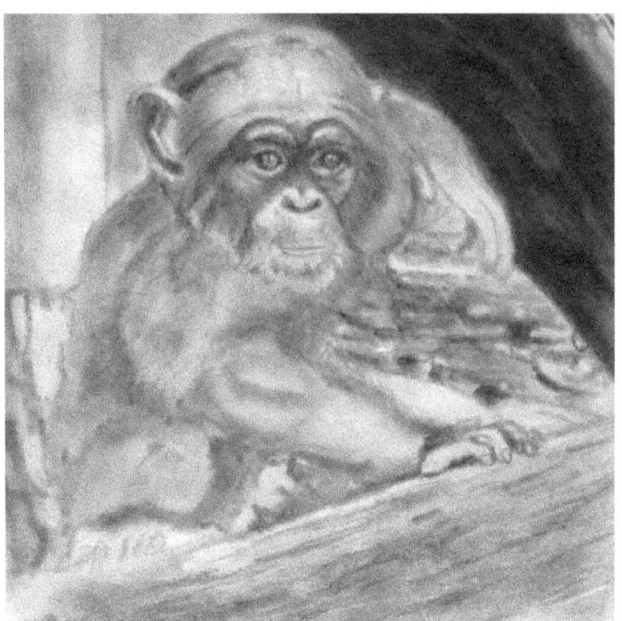

11.   For the final step: Add another coat of Soft Charcoal S. with Round brush to the entire parts lightly and don't forget to tap the brush in the container, then add the rest of the details with Hard Charcoal Pencil, Draw thin hair lines of strokes to render the hair on the arms, legs, back and the rest of the body with hair that are evident (take note that not all areas are filled with hair) and also add details on the hands and feet. Check your work for any corrections, reminder: add a tone if needed,and if you see that you applied a very dark tone to the light area erase it using your eraser.

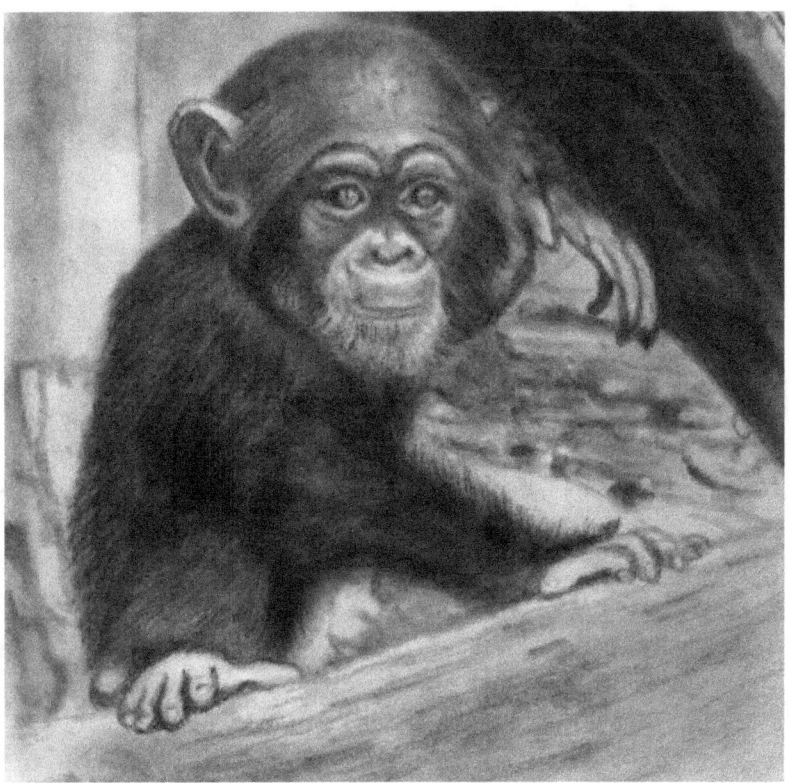

After that spray it with fixative, now it's finished and take a break, be back for the last challenge. Don't worry I'm sure you can do it.

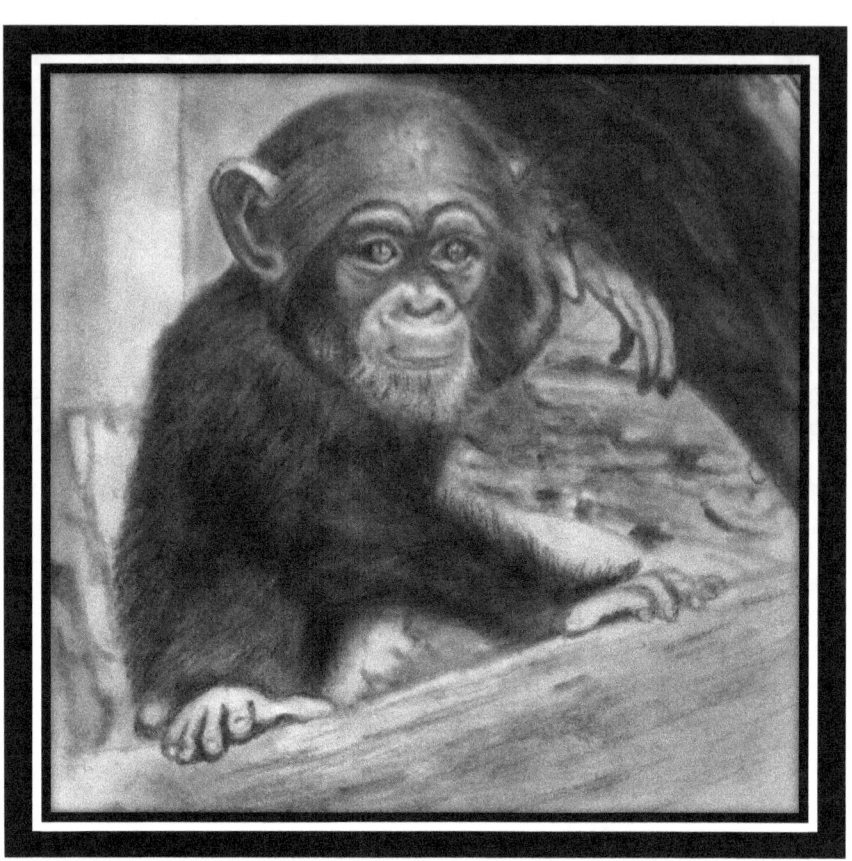

Lion

For our last exercise, we're going to render the King of the jungle, such royalty deserve a great artist to render the king and that's you. Study the picture of the Lion first, and if you ask me about the challenge it's how to render the mane and its texture, paws, grass and the rock texture in the foreground. So let's begin.

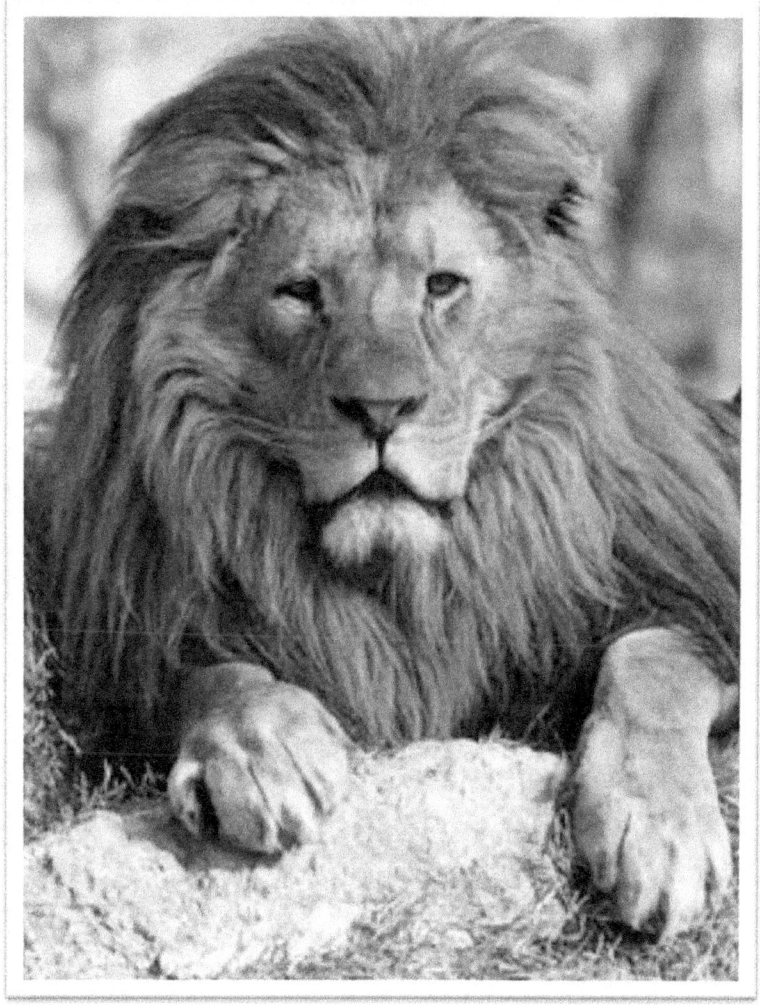

Transfer the image below to your working paper.

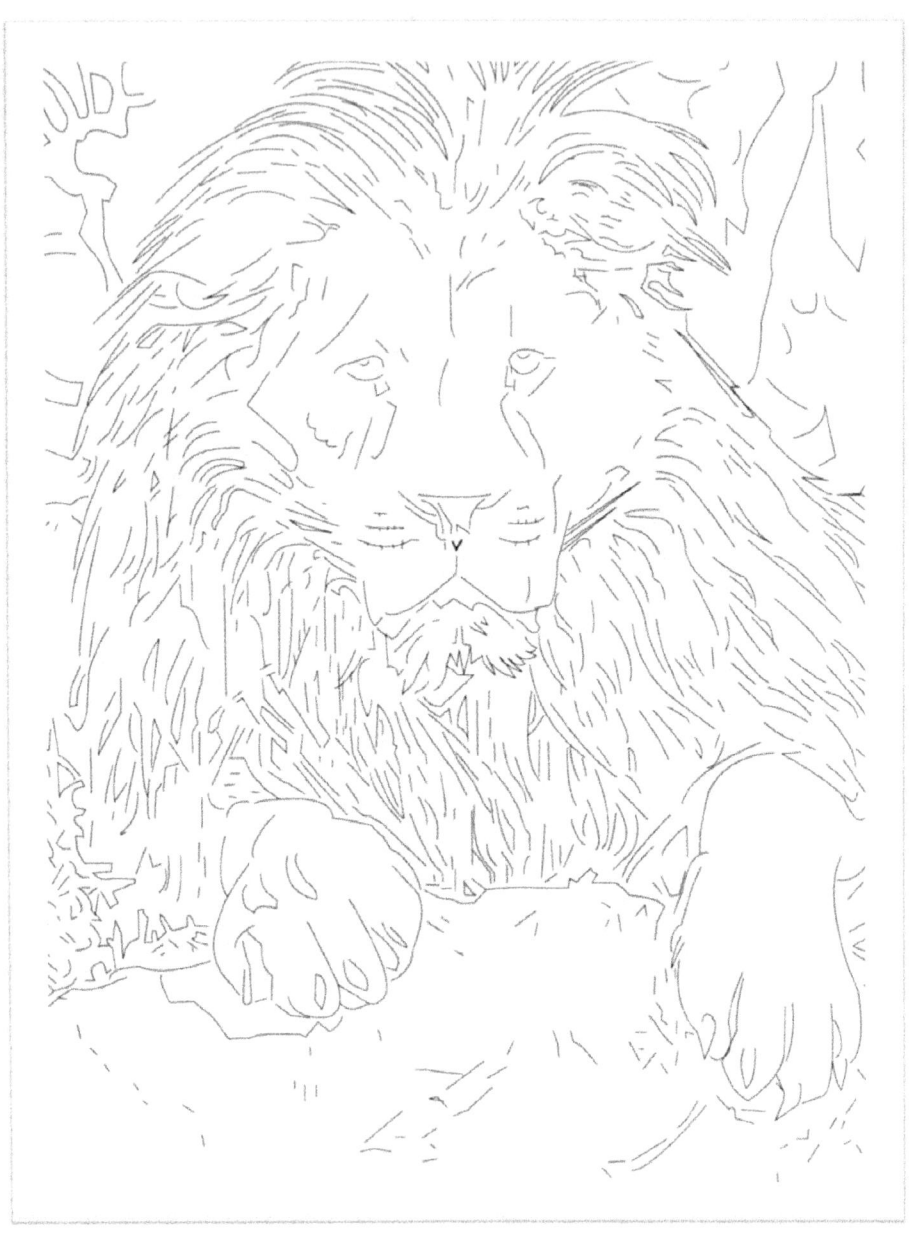

Steps:

1. As our first step start with the dark areas, let the picture below be your guide, use Soft Charcoal S. with Flat Brush.

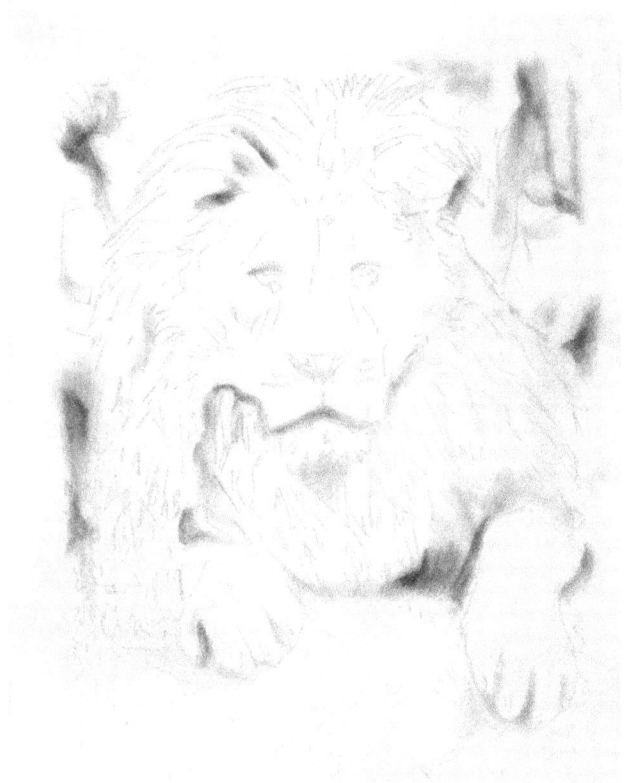

2.   Next is to use Medium Value to your work, use Medium Charcoal S. with the Flat Brush again.   Take note of the shapes, if you have a vivid imagination you can imagine it like you are making a sculpture, molding it bit by bit turning it into 3d.

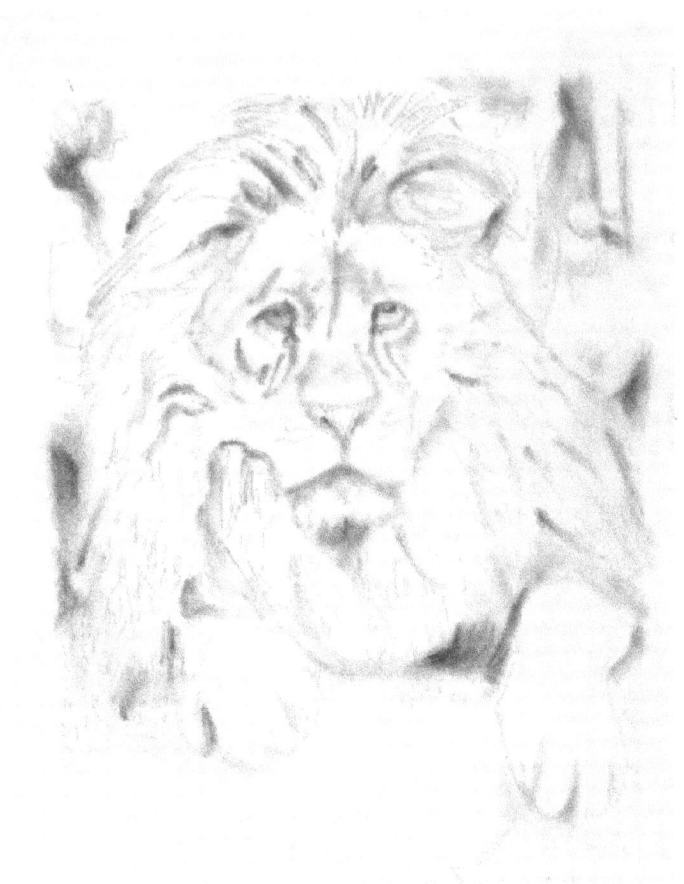

3. Continue adding the same tones and defining the shapes, notice the mane how it was rendered using the Medium Charcoal S. with Flat Brush by following the strokes of the hair flow, also the left side of the face receive less light so you have to add more tone on that side, shade the details on the parts on the face: eyes, nose and mouth.

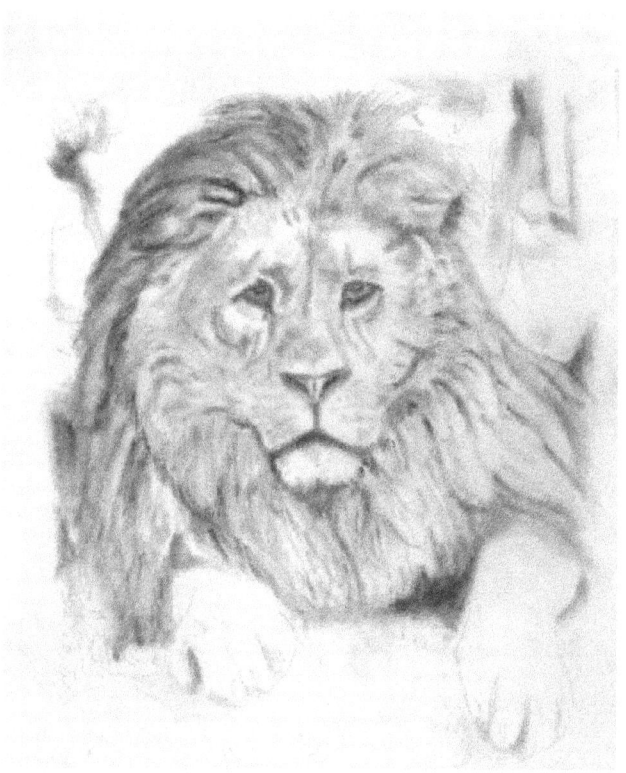

4.   Add more value to the outer mane to look more bulky, render the paws again using Medium Charcoal S. with Flat Brush, and don't forget to render the shadow with the same Charcoal.

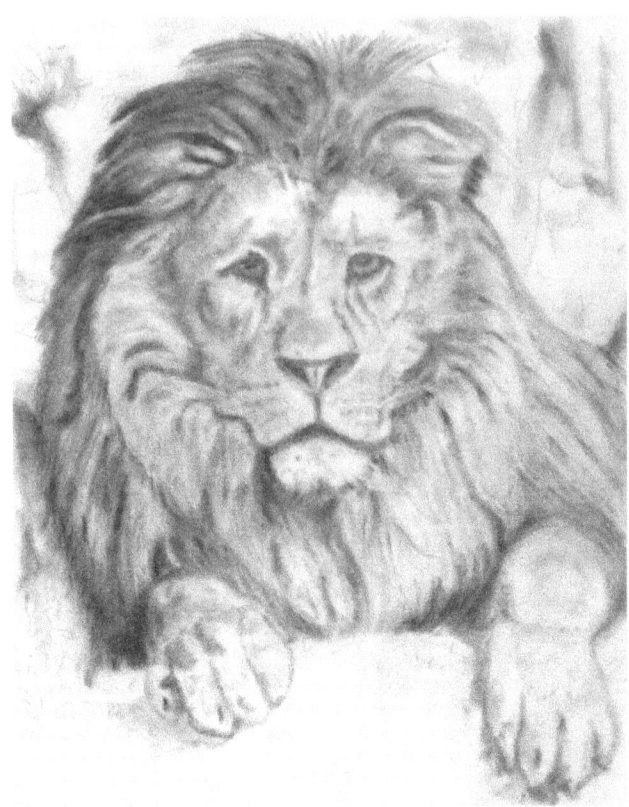

5. Last step is to render the background and foreground:
   a) Background- Shade the left side with Soft Charcoal S. with varying pressure when using your flat brush, the same thing on the right side.
   b) Foreground- For the grass use Soft Charcoal S. with Flat Brush and also with Soft Charcoal Pencil for details, also highlights was added to create a good effect.
   c) For the rock –Just use your Soft Charcoal Pencil to draw some detail lines and soften it with Tortillon, add dots with the Charcoal pencil, and add a tone on the rock with Hard Charcoal S. with Round Brush, apply slight highlights.

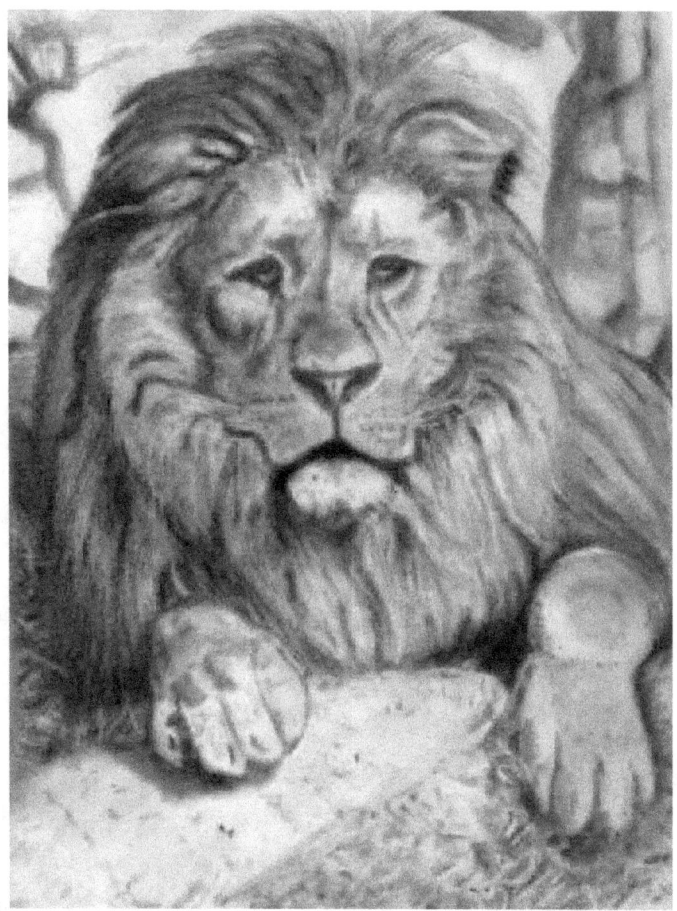

Check for any corrections if any, now we are almost finished, but first I want you to sign your Signature at the bottom of your work, as a sign of your accomplishment and finishing all the exercises, and time to spray it with fixative after that you can frame it, and hang it in your wall. - "Congratulations" you are now a great artist. Thanks for finishing this journey, and apply the new artistic skill for your benefit and also to all that surrounds you.

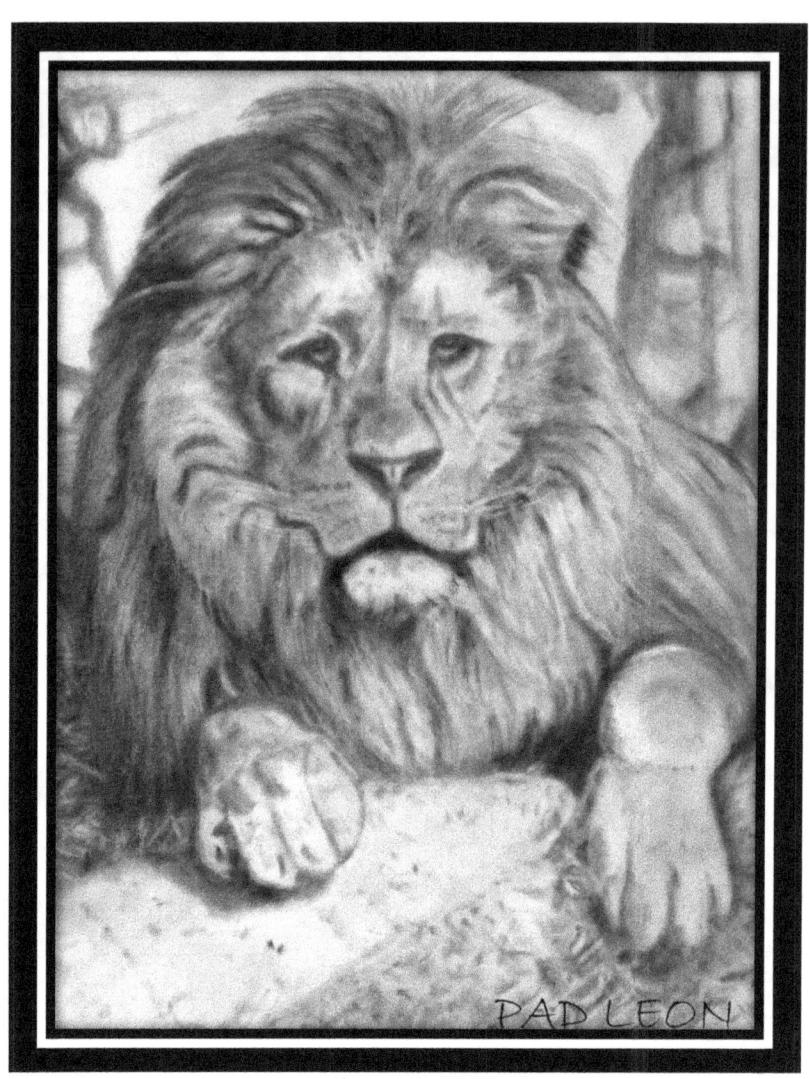

My Advice
Practice! Practice! Practice!
Thank you for reading
And Read more.

Get a copy of my other books and don't forget to read some other titles Learn How to Draw Books for the Absolute Beginner.

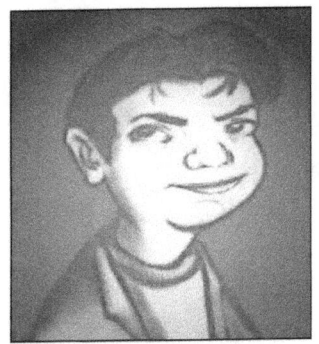

Author Bio

Paolo A. Lopez de Leon
A self taught Portrait Artist and Digital Illustrator, Experience in painting and drawing for more than 15 years. His works in various media like Pencil, Charcoal, Gouache, Watercolor, Acrylic (including Air Brush), Oil and Digital Painting. He lives in Laguna,Philippines.

This book is published by

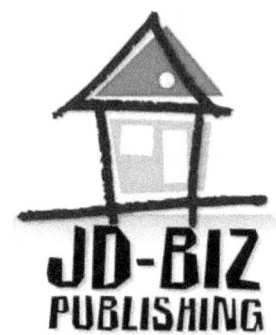

JD-Biz Corp

P O Box 374

Mendon, Utah 84325

http://www.jd-biz.com/

Read more books from John Davidson

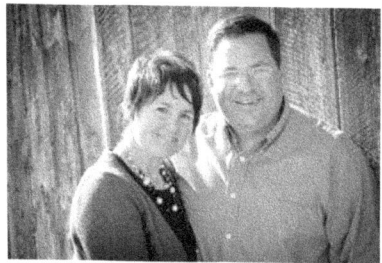

Amazon.com Author Link

Read our other books on Amazon.com

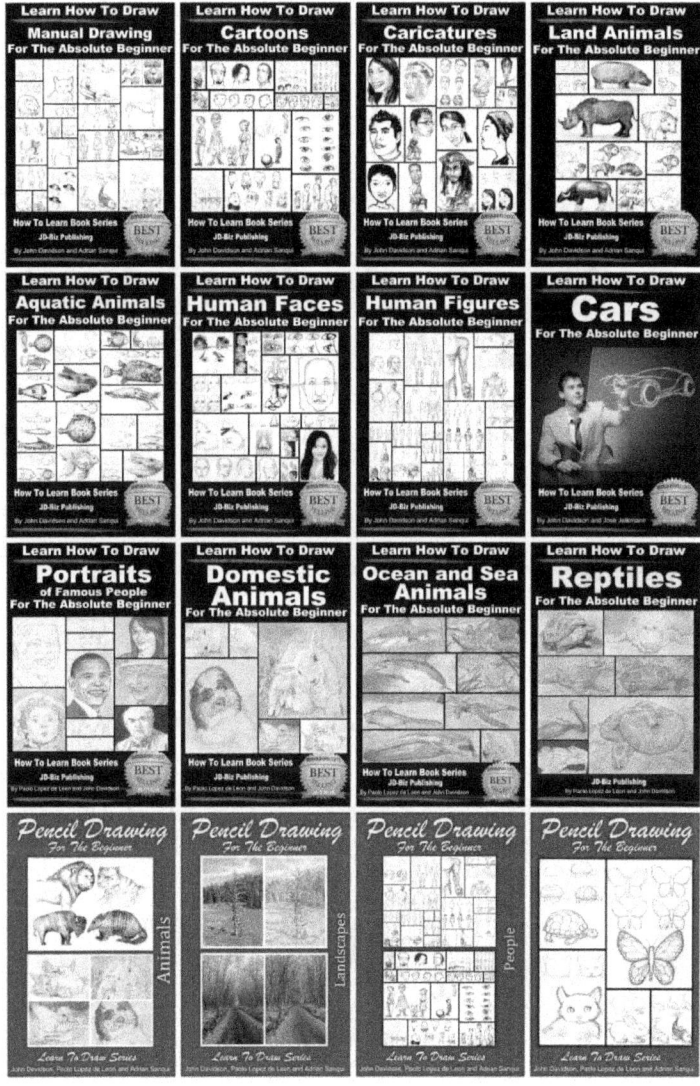

www.ingramcontent.com/pod-product-compliance
Lightning Source LLC
Chambersburg PA
CBHW070818180526
45168CB00002B/666